DR. G. M. LONGFIELD
4 Alderway Avenue S.W.
BRAMPTON   —   ONTARIO

Murder in the Yukon

Murder in the Yukon: The Case Against George O'Brien

M. J. Malcolm

Western Producer Prairie Books
Saskatoon, Saskatchewan

Printed and bound in Canada by Modern Press ⟿1
Saskatoon, Saskatchewan

Cover design by Warren Clark, GDL

Western Producer Prairie Books publications are produced and manufactured in the middle of western Canada by a unique publishing venture owned by a group of prairie farmers who are members of Saskatchewan Wheat Pool. Our first book in 1954 was a reprint of a serial originally carried in *The Western Producer,* a weekly newspaper serving Western Canadian farmers since 1923. We continue the tradition of providing enjoyable and informative reading for all Canadians.

Canadian Cataloguing in Publication Data

Malcolm, Murray, 1944-
    Murder in the Yukon

    Bibliography: p.
    ISBN 0-88833-096-0

    1. Murder — Yukon Territory — Case studies.
2. Trials (Murder) — Yukon Territory.
3. O'Brien, George.   4. North West Mounted
Police (Canada).   I. Title.
HV6535.C32Y85   364.1'523'097191   C82-091177-1

For Marianne and Keith

Contents

Contents

Acknowledgments

I want to thank Public Archives Canada for assistance in this project. I am especially grateful for permission to reproduce photographs and documents from Public Archives Canada, Records of the Royal Canadian Mounted Police, RG 18, volume 253, file 318, pt. 2 and PAC, RG 18, volume 254, file 318, pt. 4.

The staff of the Yukon Archives, of the University of Washington Press, and of the Public Libraries in both Regina and Saskatoon were most helpful and I offer them my thanks.

I am grateful to Mr. S. Horrall, RCMP Historian, who kindly supplied biographical information on Inspector Scarth, Corporal Ryan, and Constable Pennycuick.

Finally, I want to acknowledge my indebtedness to Ed McCann and Malcolm Wake, whose generosity helped get the project started; to Don Klancher, whose efforts helped keep it going; to Edith Malcolm, whose encouragement helped me finish it; and to Isobel Findlay, whose suggestions greatly improved the final product.

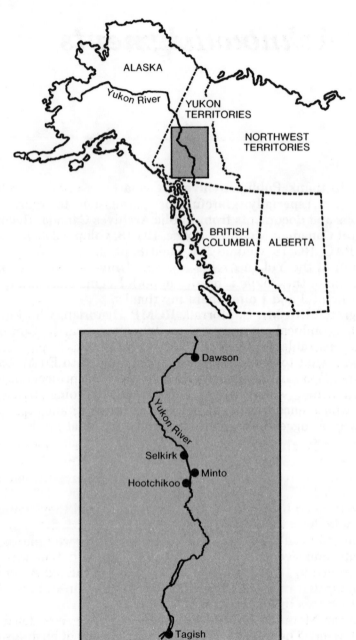

Map 1

Introduction

This is a detective story. It concerns a crime which was, in the words of Frederick C. Wade, "the most diabolical . . . probably ever committed on this continent." Since Mr. Wade was the lawyer who prosecuted the case and the words are from his opening remarks to the jury, he can, perhaps, be forgiven a measure of overstatement. Nonetheless, the case *was* remarkable.

It took place in the Yukon Territory at the end of the Gold Rush. The Klondike spawned hundreds of stories, some of them factual, many of them fictional, all of them fantastic. Almost any story originating in the Yukon in the years 1896 to 1900 was assured wide circulation. The world, it seemed, was hungry for them. The tale of the cold-blooded murder of three men on their way from Dawson to the outside made great copy — blood and gold are a heady mixture. And the story was all the more pathetic because the victims — well-liked and esteemed in Dawson — were so callously cut down on Christmas Day.

The fact that the crime was murder was, in itself, remarkable. Murders were exceedingly rare in the Yukon. The Gold Rush brought with it a great deal of petty crime — theft, prostitution, and the like. N.W.M.P. Inspector Constantine wrote, in 1897, "Heretofore goods could be cached at the side of trails and they would be perfectly safe. Now a man has to sit on his cache with a shotgun to ensure the safety of his goods. Cabins in out-of-the way places are broken into and everything cleaned out." This situation was not much improved in 1899. But murders, the stuff of the old American West and, for that matter, of Skagway, were all but unheard of. And the credit for this belongs to the N.W.M.P.

It was the Mounted Police who shepherded travelers down the river to Dawson. The Police enforced Sunday closing of business and regulated prostitution for the sake of decency. And it was a police order that prohibited guns in Dawson. That rule, more than any other, maintained the peace of the town.

There were complaints, of course, from those whose experience in California and Alaska led them to think there was something stifling about a mining town in which law and order prevailed. They soon became accustomed, however, to living in a territory in which their lives were not in constant danger and most of them even learned to like it. In fact, when three men disappeared from the trail in the winter of '99, there was an immediate uproar. After the event there was to be much self-congratulatory talk in the newspapers of calm and trust in the Police, but at the time feelings ran high. Fears amounting to hysteria were betrayed in popular reports of the period. Questions were asked: Where were the Mounted Police? Why didn't they know where the men were? Things had come to a pretty pass when a man couldn't travel the river trail without being waylaid. Or had the men simply set off up some creek in pursuit of the latest gold rumor? Why did the police not know? It was, after all, expected that the Mounted Police should know the comings and goings of thousands of people, whether in the turmoil of Dawson or on the hundreds of miles of bush and river trail. They had done it for three years. Their rules were obeyed absolutely and the gold rush had been as orderly as such a venture is ever likely to be. But when the three men disappeared, it was as if the police were being deliberately sneered at, defied. Their supremacy was being challenged and that could not be tolerated. If the matter of the missing men could not be satisfactorily explained, the reputation of the police would suffer; much of what they had accomplished would be lost. Even worse, if the idea became commonplace that their grip was slipping, they were in danger of being overwhelmed by sheer numbers. So, this case, above all others, had to be solved — visibly solved. No effort would be too great; no price too high.

It is the police work, above all else, that makes the O'Brien case remarkable. The investigation covered the three hundred-odd miles of trail which twisted from Dawson to Tagish, following the Yukon River. That trail, in the winter of 1899, was reasonably well-established. Thousands of people had been over it since the discovery of gold in 1896. There were roadhouses every fifteen or twenty miles and this ready availability of food and shelter made the traveler's life a little easier. But, it was still a rough trail snaking through hundreds of square miles of rock and bush and river, territory which, in winter, was as inhospitable as any place on earth.

The search finally focused on a few hundred yards of the trail, most of it in the bush on the banks of the Yukon, between Minto and

Hootchikoo. It was there that for almost six months, the Mounted Police scratched over the ground, looking for the bits of physical evidence from which a murder case would be built. To get some appreciation of this task, I invite the reader to imagine himself in the following situation. He is standing at one end of five blocks of sidewalk. The sidewalk is covered by thirty inches of snow. Buried somewhere in the snow is the ignition key to his car and it must be found — it is the only one he has. Formidable task.

The job that faced the Mounted Police detectives was even more difficult. The ground was rough, covered with dead weeds and brush and trees. And, of course, they did not know what they were looking for; they were simply searching for any physical evidence that might be present, hoping to deduce from that evidence details of what had happened there weeks before. It is the story of that search which I present here.

My first concern was that the story be accurate. Accordingly, I relied on the transcript of the trial of George O'Brien for the final word on exactly what had been found, where it was found, who found it and when. It was usually clear, too, what significance each piece of evidence had been assigned by the police.

Starting from these facts, I have reconstructed the story of the investigation and trial so that the reader can, I hope, feel something of the atmosphere in which they were carried out. To do this, I have invented rather freely. With the exception of the fictional Albert Ash, Nick, and Thompson, however, I have used the original participants under their own names. But I do not, for example, *know* what conversations took place, I do not know precisely how Philip Maguire, a freelance American detective, came to be employed by the N.W.M.P., I do not know why the police in Dawson asked that George O'Brien be detained in Tagish on suspicion of cache theft. To fill these gaps, I have invented conversations, situations, and explanations. I cannot, of course, claim the inventions are factual but they are, I hope, plausible.

Fewer inventions were required in the reconstruction of the trial which was fully reported in the *Daily Klondike Nugget*. Yet, even here, there was uncertainty. The *Nugget* was lavish in its praise of the jury and the speed with which it was chosen. "The shirking tendency was not predominant. . . . They are an unusually intelligent sextette and there can be no doubt that they will try the case as sworn to do, well and truly." George O'Brien was not so impressed with the objectivity or integrity of the citizens of Dawson. He originally elected for trial by judge alone, fearing that he would not receive a fair trial by jury, such was the prejudice against him in the public mind.

Whether the jury was prejudiced or not, the case for the prosecutor proved decisive. And O'Brien could find no solace in Judge Dugas' treatment, unsympathetic as he was to defense's arguments.

One could suspect further that the defense was less effective than it might have been. Certainly O'Brien's lawyer thought him "degenerate"; he said as much, but only after the trial. But, it is not clear whether these personal feelings affected his work on O'Brien's behalf.

What is clear is that O'Brien faced formidable opponents: indeed, as Bleeker commented, he was one man against two governments. At a time when a Mounted Police constable was paid less than a dollar a day, tens of thousands of dollars were available to solve the murders of Clayson, Relfe, and Olsen.

In the end, however, there remained questions unanswered by the costly investigation and trial proceedings. Nor could I offer satisfactory solutions. For instance, it is clear from testimony that, near Minto, the Dalton Trail is on the east side of the river; all other sources I have seen place the Dalton Trail on the west side exclusively.

There are other questions, too. Did George O'Brien have a partner-in-crime? O'Brien, as Miller, was frequently seen in the company of one Graves (otherwise known as Ross) in early December 1899, with their all too memorable dogs. They were last seen together by William Powell between 16 and 19 December. When next sighted, on 27 December by Jennie Prather, O'Brien was alone. What became of his partner? Was he murdered and put under the ice of the Yukon River? Or was his the bullet-riddled body found in the bush in the spring? Or did he simply walk out of the territory, unencumbered by the bad luck that ensnared O'Brien?

And what of the nugget, the peculiar trap-door nugget that Lynn Relfe carried? Where did it go? Did O'Brien manage to sell it or is it still lying on the bank of the Yukon River where he threw it. A small matter, but it would be interesting to know for sure.

1
Christmas Eve

On the morning of Christmas Eve 1899, Lawrence Olsen and Constable William Buxton took their breakfast at the long plank table at Fussell's roadhouse in Minto. Agnes Fussell was busy dishing meat and potatoes and mush. She hummed cheerily as she poured coffee into mugs and set them before the two men.

"There you are," she said, smiling maternally. "A good cup of coffee to get you started. And I will have the rest of your meal for you in just a twinkling." She turned back to the roaring iron stove.

Buxton, lips pursed, sipped at the steaming cup, made a wry face, then sniffed the black liquid. He looked up at Olsen. "What in the name of Heaven is this?" he whispered. Olsen shook his head and touched a finger to his lips.

"And here, gentlemen . . . is your meal," said Mrs. Fussell as she returned to the table, a platter in one hand and an enormous bowl in the other. "Or should I say, *our* meal. The Captain ate earlier, and ate like a bird, as usual. Oh, I *don't* know how he does his work, eating as little as he does. But I have been *so* busy this morning, I haven't had a bite. I *do* hope you won't mind if I eat with you." She smiled again, her face flushed prettily from the heat of the cookstove. She reminded one of nothing so much as a wren, always busy, always twittering. She was as plump and quick as her husband was gaunt and slow. "You *don't* mind do you Mr. Olsen? — Constable?"

"Not a bit, Miz Fussell. Happy to have your company," said Olsen.

Buxton mumbled something unintelligible and gazed forlornly at the grayish, glutinous mass in the bowl Mrs. Fussell had set on the table.

"How very *kind* of you. Now, please, gentlemen, help yourselves to mush if you care for it. I am *sure* you will find it to your taste. I make it just as my mother did, and her mother before her. I boil it long and slow with just a pinch of salt. Oatmeal is just the thing for breakfast, I always say. Constable, please go ahead." She pushed the bowl closer to Buxton.

"Oatmeal, you say? Yes'm, I like oatmeal," he said. He looked doubtfully at the bowl, then at Mrs. Fussell who was serving herself an astounding quantity of fried meat and potatoes, then at Olsen. Olsen gestured at the bowl and nodded. Buxton dug out a piece of the gray solid and passed the large bowl across the table to Olsen who took as small a portion of the mush as he could manage, quickly drowned it in canned milk and sugar, and began to eat.

"Do you gentlemen have work to do today?" asked Mrs. Fussell as she attacked her breakfast with surprising gusto.

"Yes'm. There's some problem up the line somewhere. Maybe some bush tangled in it or something. We'll find it, though."

"I am *sure* you will, Mr. Olsen. The telegraph line must be kept up — it is the very *lifeline* of the Territory. I said that to the Captain only yesterday. The telegraph is the lifeline of the Territory, I said. And the Captain could not but agree. I am sure it is of immense help to the Police, too."

"Yes ma'm . . . immense," said Buxton, swallowing hard.

"Can I expect you gentlemen at my table tonight?"

"We could be late," said Olsen. "But we'll be back. I wanted to get this trouble fixed today so we could take it easy on Christmas Day. So we'll be out as long as necessary today."

"Well I *do* hope I can count on you to be our guests for Christmas dinner. I am planning a marvelous meal. Mr. Olsen, you will remember I invited you over a week ago. I do hope you will agree to stay. And, Constable, I hope you will join us."

"I'm sorry, Miz Fussell," said Olsen. "I'll be going down to Hootchikoo on Christmas Day. I meant to tell you before."

"I'm on duty in Selkirk on the twenty-fifth," said Buxton, hurriedly. "But thanks for asking."

"Oh my. *How* disappointing. But, of course, I understand that duty must come before pleasure. If you can make it, though — by some chance — please come. There will be plenty for everyone."

"Thank you, Miz Fussell," said Olsen, as he spooned up the last of the syrupy milk from his dish. He pushed back his chair. "And speaking of duty — I must get along."

"Right," Buxton said, scrambling to his feet. "The sooner we're out, the sooner we're back."

"But, gentlemen," Mrs. Fussell protested. "You have had no

meat or potatoes. And let me get you more coffee. You cannot go out
on the trail half-fed."

"We really must go. I'll just gather my tools from the bunkhouse
and we'll be on our way." At that, Olsen left the dining room with
Buxton close behind mumbling something about helping with the
tools. Agnes Fussell looked at the breakfast, mostly untouched,
sighed, and served herself another slab of fried beef from the
congealed tallow in the platter.

The winter trail was in fine shape, well-beaten and, in most
places, wide enough for the two men to walk abreast. But it was a
twisting trail, following the course of the Yukon River. Most of the
time, it was on the ice, which was still smooth, but, later in the
winter when the ice and snow would pile in great hummocks and the
running water would undermine the ice leaving patches of open
water, the course of the trail would change. Sometimes it would
swing wide to avoid treacherous ice, sometimes it would climb the
bank and meander through the bush to avoid a rough spot or,
perhaps, to cut a half-mile off the hundred and fifty miles to Dawson.

Mostly, the telegraph line ran parallel to the trail but, because
neither the line nor the trail was straight, they were sometimes a
goodly distance apart. And that meant that Olsen and Buxton spent
their morning wallowing in deep snow, breaking their own trail to
check a stretch of inaccessible line, then cutting back to the packed
trail whenever it was possible. By noon, they had found the problem:
a sagging deadfall was tangled in the wire. The wire was not broken
but was stretched like a fiddle string with the weight of the dead
tree. The two men floundered off the packed trail and made their
way to the line.

"That'll be it," said Olsen. "The wire's not busted but she'll be
shorting out now and then." He pulled off his mitts and stuck both
hands inside the neck of his parka, against the bare skin. "You can
start cutting down there at the butt. I'll try to free the wire so I can
pull it up tight after we drag the wood off it." Buxton nodded and
the ice-rime on his hood rattled softly.

The two men went to work at a measured pace, axes swinging
with fluid economy despite the encumbrance of parkas and thick
mitts. They worked slowly for to rush was to sweat. And sweaty
clothes could mean disaster; a man could freeze in an hour. It would
happen swiftly, painlessly and, by the time he or his partner realized
what was happening, parts of his body would be dead.

By just after three in the afternoon, the job was done. They had cut back the wood and hauled the branches off. Olsen pulled some slack out of the wire, replaced an insulator, and spiked the pin back in place. They gathered their tools and began the walk back to Minto.

As Buxton and Olsen began their return trip to Fussell's from the south, two other men were approaching the roadhouse from the north. Both men had come from Dawson; both were heading for their homes outside. They were Lynn Relfe and Fred Clayson.

Relfe had left Dawson on 16 December looking forward to a long-delayed visit with his family in Seattle. The days before his departure had been hectic. There were parties to attend, goodbyes to be said and, it seemed, half the people in Dawson had messages they wanted Relfe to deliver for them on his way out. Several had letters ready for him to carry and he collected them. A friend wanted a dozen of Dr. Burner's Catarrh Cure, there being none to be had in Dawson, and Relfe wrote the order in his notebook. He had the bank issue a draft for the $1350 that he wanted to take along and, for the expenses of meals and bunks along the way, he took some Canadian currency. The remainder of his cash — $100 — he had changed into American currency for use in Skagway. Murray Eads, owner of the Pavilion, always had plenty of American notes and he was glad to exchange them for Relfe's Canadian money.

After several days of such organizing, Relfe was sure he had everything taken care of but, on the night of 15 December he stopped into the Pavilion where he had once worked as cashier and bookkeeper. There George Noble pounced. He had heard that Relfe was leaving for the outside and he, too, had favors to ask. The letter Noble wanted to send was not yet written but he promised to have it ready first thing in the morning. When Relfe and his good friend, Abe Ritzwaller, came back the next morning at half past six, the letter still wasn't ready. It had been a busy night at the Pavilion and, even at this hour, Noble was still doing his accounts. However, he quickly scribbled the letter and gave it to Relfe. In addition, he had an odd nugget — something of a collector's piece — which he wanted carried out. Relfe took it, too.

Lynn Relfe was almost ready to leave. He had the money he needed, he had all the letters for delivery, and he had several short messages in his notebook. And he had George Noble's nugget. A solid breakfast was all he needed now — Ritzwaller insisted upon that. He said that Relfe still looked gaunt from the typhoid in

August. What with that and the hours he kept at the Pavilion, it was no wonder he looked poorly. Ritzwaller paid for breakfast in the cafe next door. By a quarter to eight, Relfe was on his way out of Dawson, traveling light with only a knapsack slung over his shoulder. The morning was fine. Ritzwaller walked along with him for four or five miles, then bade him farewell — for the last time.

Fred Clayson had left Dawson a day earlier than Relfe. He fully expected to make a fast trip because he intended to skim along the river trail on his bicycle. It was an excellent machine — 1897 Columbia — and Clayson was in high spirits as he left. He had every reason to be happy. He, too, was going home. His destination was Skagway where he and his brother, Will, were established as Yukon outfitters, a business which in the past two years had been especially profitable. During the summer, Fred had taken a scow loaded with merchandise to Dawson and had disposed of the lot at top prices. Business was good, life was good, and Fred Clayson was traveling in high style.

Even the savage cold of the Yukon winter held no terrors for him. After much discussion and thought, he had adopted the combination of garments which, he was sure, would provide him comfort. The secret was chamois underwear, the shirt of which was double-breasted and double-backed. So effective was this outfit that there was some concern that he might even be too warm. Ventilation was called for so Clayson borrowed a ticket punch from his friend and business associate, Thomas Firth, and punched vent holes through the leather in the front, the back, and the armpits. There were, he reckoned, exactly the right number of holes to keep a man from becoming clammy inside the shirt, even with the brisk exertion of cycling. It was a near-perfect arrangement.

Less than a day out of Dawson, part of Clayson's plan went awry: he broke a pedal on his bicycle. Undaunted, he carried on, albeit at a much slower pace. He wheeled the crippled bicycle along in the hope that someone, somewhere along the river, would have the tools and materials to repair it. Even this setback, however, did not dampen his high spirits. Fred Clayson was a businessman and he saw a demand to be met. A return trip to Dawson would be good business and he planned to make the trip again laden with supplies, as soon as it could be arranged. But his return to Dawson would not be as an energetic man of trade.

It was because of a broken pedal, then, that Lynn Relfe had finally overtaken Fred Clayson. The men had taken pleasure in one another's company and had, for most of the past week, traveled together. And it was thus that Clayson and Relfe happened to be coming up on Fussell's roadhouse, from the north, at four-thirty on the afternoon of Christmas Eve, 1899. They stepped smartly — Clayson as smartly as his bicycle would permit — looking forward to the warmth of the bunkhouse. And the next day, Christmas Day, perhaps there would be something special laid on that would give them a reason to stop over.

By six, Olsen and Buxton returned to an effusive welcome from Mrs. Fussell who urged them quickly to wash up for supper.

"There is your wash water, gentlemen. *Do* hurry — supper is ready. Oh, I *hope* it is not ruined," Mrs. Fussell said, taking a platter of fried beef and potatoes from the oven and placing it on the table.

"I don't know how you could tell whether it was ruined or not," Buxton whispered, as he waited his turn at the basin. Olsen looked up from the basin, his face dripping, and glared at his partner.

"Everyone else has eaten — over an *hour* ago as a matter of fact. I don't like to make a *practice* of serving at odd hours but you gentlemen *are* rather special guests. Let me just close the bunkhouse door so the chatter doesn't disturb your meal."

"Look at it. Looks just like breakfast," Buxton whispered. "Probably *is* breakfast."

"Will you be quiet?" Olsen hissed. Agnes Fussell came back across the dining room.

"Here now, Mr. Olsen ... Constable, sit and eat, please. My goodness, we certainly have a lot of guests tonight. Mr. Charleson is here. He is with the Public Works Department. Do you know him? No? And Early Woolsey is in, and Mr. Dorman, and Mr. Watson from Los Angeles. And, oh my, who *else*? Oh, yes Constable Richardson is here — you will know him." Buxton nodded. "And Mr. Clayson and Mr. Relfe are here from Dawson. They are on their way out. I hope to prevail upon them to stay with us for dinner tomorrow. It would be a *shame* to spend Christmas on the trail. When you don't *have* to, that is," she looked significantly at the two men. "Now, if you have everything, I must ask you to excuse me. I want to retire now because I must be up *very* early to prepare Christmas dinner. Henry will clear your dishes — when the Captain finds him. I bid you good night."

"Good night, Miz Fussell," said Olsen.

" 'Night," said Buxton. As soon as Agnes Fussell had left the room, Buxton placed his knife and fork in his plate and leaned forward. "What ever possessed that woman to start a roadhouse. I thought breakfast might have been an accident, but she did it again. Look at this stuff."

"It's always like this," said Olsen. "But she's such a fine woman. I wouldn't want to hurt her feelings."

"Feelings, nothing," snorted Buxton. "She's getting paid."

"I know, but still . . . Listen, forget the supper. I'll go find the Captain and get a bottle of whiskey from him. We can celebrate the season. And I can think about my Christmas dinner. Ryan asked me down to Hootchikoo — like I said this morning. He claims to have a turkey, too. I don't know if he's any good as a policeman, but he is one fine cook, that man."

Later, when Olsen had got his whiskey, he, Buxton, and Henry Darud, Fussell's hired man, sat on Olsen's bunk and drank. As a regular patron, Olsen had prior claim to one of the bunks nearest the stove.

The bunk on the other side of the stove was occupied by Lynn Relfe, the young fellow from Dawson. Olsen and his group paid little attention to Relfe but sprawled, chatting and passing the bottle. Late in the evening, however, Relfe attracted the attention of most of the guests. He was showing off George Noble's nugget, a most peculiar nugget about the size of a half-dollar. In one side of the lump of gold, there was a smaller nugget, trapped, but free to rattle about. Everyone crowded around to admire the intricate knot of gold, to heft it and poke at the loose bit. The nugget was passed from hand to hand and exclaimed over: everyone swore he had never seen its like.

Next morning Captain Fussell walked into the dark bunkhouse and picked his way among the sleeping travelers to the iron stove. He flicked the draft lever open with a clang and opened the firebox door noisily.

"Merry Christmas, boys," he roared in a voice that shook the timbers. "Breakfast in half an hour." He dug in the night's ashes, baring a bed of embers. He gently laid a handful of splinters on the coals and straightened up to give them a chance to catch. "Come on now, boys, shake a leg. You know Mrs. Fussell doesn't tolerate latecomers in her dining room." He held his lantern high, casting the light into the far corner of the room. "Henry!" he bellowed at the lump under the robes of the corner bunk. "Are you still in bed, you lazy villain? How do you expect Mrs. Fussell to do her cooking without firewood?" There was a grunt from the pile of blankets, then a sudden flurry of motion as Henry Darud scrabbled for his clothes.

The Captain set a dozen thin sticks on the blazing splinters. "Don't forget Christmas dinner," he said. He piled several split logs on the fire and kicked the firebox door shut. He fiddled with the draft until he was satisfied that the fire had caught properly then turned and strode heavily out of the bunkhouse. Henry Darud had already left.

Lynn Relfe was awake before Fussell's first call, but he had no intention of getting up before there was a decent fire on. He lay in his bunk and watched the flames flicker yellow behind the mica panels in the stove door. The bunk was only six feet from the stove and already he could feel the heat radiating against his face. Relfe reached to the small pile of personal effects on the floor by his bunk. He found his pipe in the pile but no matches. He rummaged in the pile for a moment then, muttering to himself, flung back the robes and got out of his bunk. Even with two pairs of socks on, he could feel the floorboards cold underfoot. He found a splinter in the wood box, lit it in the fire and touched the blazing stick to his pipe bowl. He sucked deeply once, twice, tamped the tobacco, sucked again, and threw the splinter into the stove. The first smoke of the day is always the best, he thought, as he puffed on his pipe and warmed himself in front of the stove.

Christmas Day, he thought. Yes, that would be right. Ten days out of Dawson — a hundred and fifty miles. That's good time but still the better part of a week to Skagway. No celebration for you this year, my lad, not with miles to be covered. Ah, but it wouldn't be like last year anyway. What a spread the Pavilion had laid on!

The heat from the stove had by now penetrated the clothes which were hung around on chairs and clothes horses. A musty aroma began to fill the room. Relfe picked a shirt and a set of drawers from one of the chairs and flung the garments across the room.

"Fred! Get up and do something with these blasted goatskin drawers of yours," he said. "The stink is going to put everybody off their breakfast."

Fred Clayson got out of his bunk and retrieved the clothes that Relfe had thrown. "Don't care if they do stink," he said. "I always maintained that chamois underclothes over a set of woollens will keep you warmer than anything else you can wear."

"Chamois is all right," Relfe replied. "But why'd you go and buy billy goat hide? I tell you, if we meet the mail driver today you'd better give his team a wide berth."

."Why?"

"Because the dogs would take turns cocking their legs on you like you were a dead fish." This triggered a shout of laughter from Olsen who was sorting his socks out of the welter of clothes. The laugh tailed off in a rasping cough.

"Sounds like a great set of lungs you got there," said Relfe. "The medicine you took last night doesn't seem to have helped much."

"It helped some," said Olsen as he walked over to the stove and spat a clot of phlegm into the fire. "But, come noon, I plan to take some more medicine right after I have my Christmas dinner."

"Here?"

"No. I'm striking out for Hootchikoo right after breakfast. I'll have a nice brisk walk to work up an appetite for Ryan's turkey."

"Ryan's? Must be a new roadhouse; I've never heard of it."

"Not a roadhouse — the Police post. Ryan's the Corporal there." Olsen turned to his bunk and picked up his parka. "Will you be staying here?"

"We haven't decided. Fred and I have a long way to go yet, but the lady's offer last night sure sounded tempting." He gestured with his thumb toward Agnes Fussell's dining room.

"I don't know if you want to stay here," said Olsen, heading for the door.

"Why not?"

"Ask Buxton," Olsen answered and walked into the black Yukon morning.

"What about it, Buxton? Mrs. Fussell said she was having turkey and that sounds good to me." Buxton looked up from the chair where he was hunched, lacing his boots.

"I've only eaten two meals here and both of them would have given a dog heartburn. Olsen is a regular and he says it's always like that. I don't even want to think about what she would do to a perfectly good turkey. She can even spoil tea — so help me, it would take the rust off a gun barrel. But what am I telling you for? You had supper here last night, didn't you? How was it?"

"Well ..."

"Right, and I'll tell you about breakfast. She'll fry beef and potatoes, just like you got for supper last night, and she'll cook them so you can't tell which piece is meat and which is spud. Or, if you want you can have mush. It'll be scorched, that's for certain, and it will have lumps in it as big as eggs."

"Ah, eggs. My kingdom for an egg," moaned Clayson.

"Lumps in the porridge are as close as you'll get to them here," said Buxton. Olsen came back into the bunkhouse, stamping the snow from his boots. He tossed his parka on the bunk and walked over to the stove, his hands held out to the warmth.

"What kind of a day we got out there?" Buxton asked.

"Maybe forty-five below," Olsen answered, briskly rubbing his hands together. "But the sky's clear." Then he turned to Relfe. "Did he tell you what Christmas dinner would be like here?"

"He did and it didn't sound very appealing. But we don't have a lot of choice. Do we, Fred?" Clayson, having finished dressing, joined the three men at the stove.

"I guess not," he said. "We ought to push on but I would like to take the day off. Oh, what's the difference? We can stay here. Even if the food is awful, we can always tap the good Captain's supply of Canadian Club. It won't be a total loss."

"Listen, why don't you come to Ryan's with me? Yes, both of you. He said he would have a turkey — where he was going to get one, I don't know and I'm not about to ask. But turkey or no, there will be lots of grub — good grub, too, like I said." Olsen looked inquiringly from Relfe to Clayson. Relfe was silent a moment, intent upon digging at his pipe bowl.

"I don't know," he said. "It sounds good, but we don't even know this fellow."

"That's no matter," said Olsen generously. "Paddy would be glad of the company. And, if you wanted to, you could bring some whiskey with you; that could be your contribution to the dinner." He was interrupted by John Fussell who pushed open the door from the dining room and bellowed, "Grub's on."

Buxton cast his eyes at the ceiling, as if calling upon Heaven to witness his martyrdom and followed the Captain into the dining room.

"Think about it," said Olsen. "I'll be leaving right after breakfast." And he went in to eat his usual breakfast of canned milk and sugar.

"Well, Fred, what do you think?"

"I say let's go with him. We cover a few miles and we get Christmas dinner too. How can we lose? I might even find somebody who can fix my bicycle."

"Forget about the cycle. We would probably be in Skagway by now if you hadn't been trundling that thing along."

"I would have been in Skagway all right, if the pedal hadn't broken." They could hear Agnes Fussell chirping about everyone needing a good cup of coffee to start the day. Relfe looked through the door to the dining room.

"We had better get in there," he said. "And she will want to know about dinner. So, it's settled then, is it? We go to Hootchi-koo?" Clayson nodded. "Good. I'll tell Olsen." And the two men hurried in to take breakfast, having made the most important decision they had ever made.

It was Christmas Day, 1899. For Clayson, Relfe, and Olsen it was the last day of their lives.

2
Christmas Day

As Clayson, Olsen, and Relfe left Minto, two mail drivers, Bayard Burgess and Joe Mercedes, were hitching their teams at Mackay's thirty miles to the south. Their sleds were heavily loaded with downstream mail and, Christmas Day or not, that mail was due at Selkirk on the twenty-sixth. So, today they would carry through Hootchikoo to Minto, leaving a mere twenty miles to Selkirk for the following day. The trail was hard, the dogs rested and fed; they would be moving fast today. Burgess planned to be in Minto by early afternoon.

He looked back at Mercedes who was finishing tying down his load. He had to shout to be heard above the chorus of whines and yelps.

"All set?" he called. Mercedes waved him on. "Let's go then — HAH!" Burgess roared at his team and, as they lunged into their harnesses, he heaved the sled from behind.

"HAH! HAH!" Burgess shouted again and, at a brisk run, swung onto the river trail, heading north into the darkness.

At the police post at Hootchikoo, Corporal Patrick Joseph Ryan sat at his table completing reports for Dawson to be sent on the downstream mail sled. He had been up since six, partly to get the mail packet ready, and also to put the turkey in the oven for dinner. He would be having guests: Olsen was coming and so were two woodcutters from a camp down river. Ryan knew them only as Thompson and Nick.

Thompson was a slim, cheerful man from some place in Ontario — Ryan could not remember where exactly. Nick, on the other hand, was something of a mystery. He was short and dark and powerful but besides that he had two outstanding features. Ryan had never heard him utter a single word. Perhaps he could not even speak English — that was possible — but his only contribution to conversation were short, sharp nods. Nick was, in addition, the most appallingly dirty human being Ryan had ever seen. That, too, was a mystery. It was not obvious how one got filthy cutting wood but Nick had managed. Certainly, dirt accounted for much of the man's swarthy appearance and it amused Ryan to imagine Nick emerging from a bath, his complexion like a Swede's and being totally unrecognizable. Nonetheless, Thompson and Nick had little enough cheer, stuck in the bush for the winter, cutting wood and stacking it by the river where it would be used, come spring, to fire the steamboats. They certainly had no turkey and Ryan felt bound to share the one he had. So, he had invited the woodcutters for Christmas dinner. They had almost wept with joy at the invitation. That is, Thompson had. Nick just nodded, sharply.

Ryan got up from his table, the mail completed, and checked the roasting bird. As he opened the oven door, a cloud of steam, fragrant with sage and onions, poured out, enveloping him. Yes, it was roasting nicely. He spread a cloth soaked in bacon drippings over the breast to keep the white meat moist and returned the turkey to the oven. As he latched the oven door, Ryan felt a tiny surge of pride in his stove. It was a fine stove, just the sort one needed to do a decent bit of cooking. It was not one of the miserable, little tin boxes that most cabins had, but a proper iron cookstove with a warming closet, a reservoir for hot water, and an ample oven. Ryan had obtained it by blind luck.

In the summer of 1898, Ryan had chanced upon a desperate-looking man who was struggling downriver to Dawson. The fellow was alone in a decrepit boat. Because the boat was grossly overloaded and leaked abominably, he was making poor time, so poor in fact that it was doubtful that he would reach Dawson before freezeup. Near Hootchikoo, the man quit. Possibly, he was just exhausted. But, it was possible, too, that he was finally struck by the sheer lunacy of packing — along with everything else — several hundred pounds of cast iron into the northern wilderness. He hurled pieces of the dismantled stove clanging onto the bank. Ryan bought the pieces for three dollars thus equipping the Police post at Hootchikoo with one of the finest stoves in the north. Ryan smiled and went outside for more wood to feed his treasured stove.

When he returned, he made a quick check of materials for his dinner. The turkey was roasting nicely. There was a small pudding ready for steaming and a pan of hard sauce needing only to be boiled. There were potatoes — good ones, not soft or frozen-sweet, peeled and standing in cold water. The tinned peas needed only to be heated. Unfortunately, there was no cranberry sauce, but Ryan had a large pot of orange marmalade. That would do instead. Finally, there was a small bag of hard candy to have with their tea. He had no liquor, not because he objected to it, but because it was outrageously expensive at the roadhouses. And liquor was a difficult item to scrounge, even for accomplished scroungers like Mounted Policemen. So there was none. But, they would make do; it would be a good dinner all the same.

At half past ten, the mail team arrived at the Hootchikoo post. Ryan, standing shivering in his open cabin door, could hear Burgess approach from a half-mile — shouting, whistling at his dogs, a steady commotion punctuated by the cut and crack of his thin black whip. Ryan never heard the racket but he remembered, sheepishly, seeing Burgess and his team for the first time.

It was in January of 1898 and Ryan was on his way to Dawson. He was new to the Yukon but he had seen teams of dogs before. Nothing had prepared him, however, for the sight of Burgess' mail team in full stride. Ryan remembered Pete, Burgess' lead dog, a powerful black and white brute of obscure origins. And he remembered the dog grinning, tongue lolling, as the long lash curled and cracked viciously around him. Ryan had been appalled at the cruelty and suggested that as the dogs appeared willing enough, it probably was not necessary to flog the poor creatures to get more from them.

Bayard Burgess had eyed the new policeman, then politely explained: "See, you don't hit the dogs with the lash — at least a civilized man don't. The whip is more for show, kind of like the way some men carry a fancy walking stick. When ol' Pete's got a good trail, he can run faster and longer than most men can follow. He don't need any urging. So, I throw out that lash to keep a rhythm, so to speak. And it helps keep me warm, too."

Burgess had waited for Ryan's reaction to the explanation, had got none. Then he had added an afterthought: "Oh, yeah, and I use it to break up dog fights. Mind you, putting a welt on a dog won't stop him if he's intent upon chawing another one. But, the whip lets me do a little something from fifteen or twenty feet away, which is about as close as I really want to get to a serious dog fight."

With a whoop, Burgess dragged his team to a stop in front of the Police cabin.

"Hoy, Paddy," he yelled, hoarsely. "Tap a tha marnin' t'ya." His greeting was always the same, delivered in what he supposed was a fair Irish accent that could be best appreciated by anyone called Paddy Ryan. The accent, in fact, was dreadful, and Ryan cringed a little whenever he heard it.

"Morning, Bayard. How's the trail?"

"Good. There's a bit of rough ice back there three or four miles. But, on average, she's fine." Burgess unlaced a corner of the cover on his sled and rummaged about in the load.

"Here we are," he said, producing a small sack. "Got a bit of mail for you today."

"All right, I'll swap you for the packet I have inside. Look, can you come in and warm? I'm going to freeze standing out here."

Burgess looked back down the trail where Mercedes' team was just in sight. He thought a moment. "Right," he said. "Joe will be here in ten minutes or so. I'll just step in until he comes by."

"He seems to be keeping up better these days," said Ryan as he motioned Burgess through the cabin door.

"Something smells good, Paddy," Burgess said. He sniffed appreciatively as he stood by the stove rubbing his hands. "Yeah," he went on, "Joe's got a pretty fair team now that he got rid of that mutt he used to have out front. Remember that lazy, foul-tempered white sucker he had? Got rid of him about a month ago. Finally, he got a big mongrel. Good dog. Just about keeps up with ol' Pete and me."

As Burgess spoke, Ryan dumped his mail sack. There were several letters for him — all obviously police business — which he tossed on the table. There were several others addressed to people who worked around Hootchikoo — or who had been there at one time. Finally, there was a package for Ryan personally. It contained three issues of the *Toronto Globe*. Ryan grinned; it was a splendid Christmas present.

Burgess, too, eyed the newspapers.

"Can I stop over here some night and read them, Paddy?" he asked.

"By all means. They'll be here," Ryan replied. "By the way, there is tea on the stove there, if you want some."

"No, thanks. I better get movin' before it snows"

"Snows? The sky is clear, for the love of Mike."

"I know, but it smells like snow coming. You go on and smile if you like but we will have snow before tomorrow noon — just wait and see if we don't."

"You are probably right, Bayard, so you had better use the trail while it is good. And don't forget my mail. Two of those reports are already late." Burgess fastened his parka and picked up Ryan's out-going mail packet.

"I've got them," Burgess said. "So long, Paddy. Merry Christmas."

"You, too. Oh, by the way, you didn't overtake Olsen on the trail down here, did you?

"The lineman? Nope, wasn't a soul on the trail. Was he supposed to be coming down from Mackay's?"

"I don't know," said Ryan. "He's to be here for dinner and I just thought you might have seen him. But since you didn't, I suppose he was at Renton or Minto last night. So when you see him, tell him to shake a leg. The turkey will be done right on time."

"I'll tell him," Burgess said as he left the cabin. Ryan heard the driver whistle and roar at his team and he was gone.

At a quarter to twelve, Ryan went outside for the third time to check for his company. There was no sign of Olsen but Thompson and Nick were struggling along the trail, hauling what looked to be fully half a cord of split wood. They had the wood stacked on a rough sled and Nick was plodding along with the sled's tow rope over his right shoulder. The sled scraped and bumped on the packed trail, spilling sticks as it did so. Thompson followed the load, now pushing, now picking up fallen sticks and restacking them. As they left the trail and moved into the softer snow, the pulling got harder. Snow began to boil up in front of the rude sled but the pace did not slacken. Nick simply leaned forward a little farther and bulled his way toward the cabin.

"Merry Christmas," Ryan called. Thompson waved, gathered up several more fallen sticks and helped heave the sled the last few feet to the cabin.

"Merry Christmas to you, Corporal. Where do you want it?" he asked.

"What, the wood?"

"Yeah, we brought you a present. You want it stacked by the corner there?"

"Well . . . yes . . that would be fine. But you didn't have to bring anything."

"Oh, I know. But we didn't have anything else — like that would add to the dinner, f'rinstance. So, we figured you could use some wood. Split it up the last couple of days." Thompson grinned and winked. "What Old Man Cochrane don't know won't hurt him."

"Well, that is very nice of you, gentlemen. Thank you."

"Don't mention it," Thompson said. "You go on inside. Me and Nick will have it stacked in a few minutes." Nick nodded, sharply. He wasn't even breathing hard.

Five minutes later and the wood cutters came in, stamping the snow from their boots.

"All done," Thompson said. He sniffed loudly. "Ah, the turkey," he sighed. "I think it is a hundred years since I last smelled roast turkey."

Nick nodded and immediately began stripping off his work clothes and hanging them up to dry. At last, when he had worked his way down to black trousers and an undershirt that was once white, he sat and pulled his boots off. Each foot came out encased in small chips and sawdust which he promptly brushed off onto the floor.

Ryan watched, dismayed, as Nick's grimy hands picked wood chips from his socks and dropped them on the cabin floor which, until five minutes ago, was neatly swept.

"There is hot water in the reservoir and the basin is there if you want to wash up," he said. Thompson dipped water for himself and, with much splashing and snuffling, began to scrub.

Nick, on the other hand, appeared not to have heard. His eye had been caught by the newspapers on Ryan's table. Delicately, almost reverently, he picked up one of the copies, then looked at Ryan.

"Go ahead," Ryan said, trying to hide his surprise. "They just came today." And he watched with some amazement as Nick, the man who never spoke, unfolded one of the newspapers and began to read, hungrily.

"Everything is ready," Ryan said. "We are just waiting on Olsen. You didn't see him on the trail?"

"Who?" asked Thompson, his voice muffled by the towel he was using.

"Olsen. The lineman from Five Fingers. He is supposed to be here." Thompson scowled thoughtfully.

"Don't think I know him. But it doesn't matter; there was nobody out where we were, was there, Nick?" Nick did not look up but carefully moistened a filthy fingertip and turned a page of the *Globe*.

"Well, I was half-expecting him to be here mid-morning. It is odd you didn't see him. The mail driver came from the south and saw nobody so Olsen must have been at Minto or Renton last night. He ought to have been on the trail with you."

"Well, me and Nick are camped a good ways off the main trail, don't forget. And maybe he got into a bottle with some of the boys at

Minto. Go to any roadhouse you like today and somebody will be raising hell and propping a stick under it."

"You may be right," Ryan said, doubtfully. "But Olsen is a steady sort."

"Ahh, it's Christmas, Corporal," Thompson said. Then he smiled. "I'll give you three to one the lineman is at Minto, working on his third hot buttered rum."

Ryan nodded. "We will give him fifteen minutes," he said.

At Selkirk, Constable Alexander Pennycuick was greasing his boots. He had had his Christmas dinner and was thankful that he was on duty for the day. That meant he could avoid the noise and foolishness that promised to take up the afternoon and most of the evening. He could man the post where it was quiet and warm; he could get his boots done; he could write some letters. And, with any luck, he might read a little.

He stretched his legs contentedly, wriggled his stockinged toes in the shimmering heat of the stove and kneaded grease into the leather of his boots.

Another strange Christmas, he thought. Quite unlike those in England and certainly unlike those in India. In India one fought the never-ending heat with punkahs and just the right mix of gin-and-anything. Here, one fights the deadly cold with whiskey and a red hot stove. And it was never difficult to find a native to swing a punkah; here one could jolly well cut one's own wood or freeze. Still, it is not such a bad spot, this Yukon Territory, if it were not for the unrelenting cold.

But, Macleod — that is the place to be. If ever one became accustomed to the Yukon winter, one could winter at Macleod in shirtsleeves. Like the Indians. Almost naked; poor ragged beggars. But, even the Indians, poisoned-drunk though they may be, and dressed in tatters, have more character about them than that stinking rabble in Skagway. Ah, yes. Macleod — perhaps in the spring.

"Excuse me." Pennycuick was jarred from his daydreaming by a chunky, pink-faced young man who had walked into the post.

"Are you Pennycuick?" he asked.

"Yes."

"I'm Ash, from Dawson. I am posted here."

"Oh, you are one of the new men. Good to have you here. I am Alex Pennycuick."

"Albert Ash." They shook hands.

"Where are the rest?" Pennycuick asked.

"The rest of what?"

"Of the new men."

"I'm the lot."

"One man? Blast! I understood we would get three. Oh, well, no matter. Glad to have you at least."

"I just got here. The sergeant — what's-his-name — sent me over to talk to you."

"He did? Did he say what was so urgent that it had to be dealt with on your holiday?"

"Oh, I don't think there was any urgency, really. I think he was just looking for something for me to do. So he sent me over here so you could tell me about the duty."

"Good grief," Pennycuick said, disgustedly. He rubbed slowly at his boot. "However, we had best do as we are told. You have spent all your time in Dawson, I take it?"

"Yes, I was posted there in the summer. It keeps you busy there picking up the vags and drunks. Not very exciting but it got the wood cut, I suppose."

"Yes, well, you will find that will change; you can cut your own wood here. And you may carry mail and you will travel with the telegraph man if you are needed."

"There was some talk about thefts around here," Ash said.

"Hmm, quite," Pennycuick said. "We have had a number of cache thefts. Not surprising, really. Scows loaded with goods are scattered along the river where they were trapped at freezeup. They are often unguarded — an open invitation to thieves. What is surprising, I suppose, is that there are as few thefts as there are."

"Have you any notion who the thieves are?"

"Yes I do, as a matter of fact. About two weeks ago, I missed the two I believe are responsible."

"How did that happen?"

"Just a streak of ill luck, really. We had been plagued with thefts all fall — well, from freezeup on, you understand. It was not until the eleventh or the twelfth, however, that I spotted a fellow who seemed a likely suspect."

"That was the eleventh of December?"

"Yes. This character was in Anderson's road house at the beef cache. He claimed to be a prospector, but he was trying to sell canned milk to Anderson. Now that seemed to be a strange thing for a prospector to be doing so I questioned him."

"You thought he was robbing caches and selling the goods."

"That is right. When I questioned this fellow, he got quite surly, saying it was none of my damned business where he got the milk."

"Did you know him?"

"No. He told me his name was Miller and that his partner's name was Ross. The story was that the partner had founded Rossland, British Columbia."

"Did he actually claim that himself?"

"Not to me, but to others, apparently. Sheer nonsense of course. If one took Miller and Ross together, they had neither the intelligence nor the initiative to build an outhouse, much less a town. Theirs was as miserable a camp as I have ever seen."

"You were at their camp, then?"

"Yes, such as it was. They were camped down near Hell's Gate, tucked behind a pile of cordwood. They had very little gear — and most of that stolen, I should say. And, of course, they were burning the wood that others had cut."

"This Miller fellow, what did he look like?" Constable Ash pulled out a small notebook and a stump of pencil.

"There is not much to him," Pennycuick replied. "About middling height, medium weight, dark hair and eyes. He was unshaven although I think that was more a matter of personal slovenliness than design. His partner was of about the same height but of lighter build. They had two dogs — one a yellow and white St. Bernard, the other a small black. The big fellow may have been a good worker but I think his wind was broken. The black was a silly, yapping creature. Quite useless, I should say. He probably could not pull the hat from your head."

Ash was diligently taking down the descriptions of the two men. Pennycuick craned his neck to look unobtrusively at the pages of the notebook and saw them filled with a tight, precise script. He smiled.

"Is there any further description?" Ash asked, looking up.

"No. There is nothing that really distinguishes them physically. But Miller would be easy to recognize although it is a feeling one gets about him that is memorable, as opposed to his appearance. I would surmise, for example, that he has seen the inside of more than one prison. I do not know that for a fact, mark you, but I do know he is a very sullen individual when he is in the presence of the police."

"Did you find out were they are from — assuming we discount the Rossland story."

"Not accurately. But, they are both Englishmen, as much as I hate to admit it."

"So, how did they manage to elude you?"

At this Pennycuick's eyebrows raised slightly and he sat forward in his chair.

"They did not elude me, precisely," he said, stiffly. "When I met these men, I had suspicions about how they had come by their gear, but I had no solid evidence. So, I simply stirred them up a little and left — I like to have their kind thinking they are being watched. But, they did not escape."

"Sorry, Alex," Ash said, innocently. "I didn't mean to suggest you had been sloppy."

"Fair enough. To go on, then, after I left the two men, I came back here. Then, on the fourteenth, a warrant for their arrest came from down river. Someone had better evidence than I had, obviously. But when I returned to the Hell's Gate camp with the warrant, Miller and Ross were long gone."

"Do you suppose they went out?"

"One could hope so. Certainly, if they traveled at all quickly, they could be in Skagway by now. But, I rather doubt if they are gone. We have had several thefts since and, even after catching that vagabond, Fortier, the thefts have not been eliminated."

"Well, if you are right, we ought to be able to locate these men by simply working our way south, checking every camp we found for stolen goods — and for the thieves, of course. Could that be done?"

"It would be a big job but, yes, I think it can be done. Perhaps with you here, a man could be spared to do it. I would very much like to meet Mr. Miller again. I dislike thieves and liars, especially when they are Englishmen."

"I could get started today," Ash said, eagerly.

"Good Heavens, man, don't be ridiculous. Enjoy your Christmas — or what little of it remains. There are a few books and newspapers in the cupboard over there. You can stay here where it is quiet and read if you like. Or go join the party if that is your taste. But tomorrow will be quite early enough to start after our thieves."

3
O'Brien Appears

Clayson, Relfe, and Olsen were not the only travelers on the river in December 1899. Most nights, Fussell's bunkhouse was full, or nearly so. Many of these customers, of course, were regulars: mail drivers, freighters, and, like Lawrence Olsen, telegraph men. But there were others, like Clayson and Relfe, who were on their way to or from Dawson and who might stay at a particular roadhouse only once. Albert Gibson was such a traveler. He and his party — just two days behind Clayson and Relfe — were heading for Skagway too.

Albert Gibson lived in Dawson and he owned a horse and sled. Early in December, he was approached by Ralph Bard who was willing to pay the price of a ride to the outside. Just out of Dawson, the men overtook Mr. and Mrs. Prather who, with three dogs and a sled, were traveling out, and they agreed to travel together. Gibson agreed because he had serious reservations about Mrs. Prather's ability to make the trip. She was a strong-willed woman, no doubt of that, but it was a grueling journey, certainly not one a woman ought to undertake. And Gibson was not impressed with what he saw of the Prathers' dogs. They were a poor team and, whatever the original idea was, Gibson was sure Mrs. Prather would do very little riding. She would be walking most of the way to Skagway. With Gibson's horse and sled at hand, she would be able to ride at least part of the time and thus conserve her strength.

None of the four was in any great hurry and the trip went smoothly until just north of Minto. There, to Gibson's consternation, his horse went lame and had to be left behind.

Bard and Gibson piled some of their gear on Prather's dog sled and the group continued. They reached Fussell's roadhouse on December 26.

The next morning, Gibson and Bard were up early and ready to leave but the Prathers lagged. Gibson was not surprised. He had watched the fatigue building in Mrs. Prather and, on this morning, she was in a foul mood, clearly dreading another day on the trail. And their dogs chose this particular morning to be even more cantankerous than usual. There ensued a quarter of an hour's tussle, in which the dogs snapped and yanked and tangled the traces, before they were hitched and ready to go. Jennie Prather stood shivering, watching the scene with growing anger. Gibson could see that several times she was on the verge of speaking sharply about the delay. If they were going to waste time, she wanted to waste it in the roadhouse, out of the cold. But, she said nothing and when the dogs at last took the river trail, Mrs. Prather set her jaw and followed.

All went well for about two hours. The trail was good despite the recent snow and, for once, Mr. Prather and his dogs set a brisk pace. They would be at the Hootchikoo roadhouse for the noon meal. From Minto, the trail ran hard by the right bank, following the twists and irregularities, never more than a few hundred yards from shore. About halfway to Hootchikoo, a large point of land jutted into the river. It was one of several such points but, because of numerous small islands at that point, the ice was rough for about two miles. The main trail continued on the river but its route had been changed several times and would be changed several more times before the winter was over.

Early in the winter, William Powell and his crew had encountered this stretch of bad ice. But, where travelers on foot, or with light sleds, could make their way through, Powell and his men were stopped. They were driving sleds heavily loaded with pork destined for Dawson and, after nearly losing one team in the treacherous ice, Powell decided to go overland. He left the river and cut a trail through the bush of the point. This trail rejoined the river some three miles farther on and, after Powell had used it, it was all but abandoned, useful only because it gave some access to the telegraph line.

When the Prathers and their dogs reached the point at which Powell's cutoff branched from the main trail, the dogs, unaccountably, turned off the river onto the poor track that led overland. Albert Gibson watched with some dismay as the Prathers struck up the snow-choked trail.

"Hi, there!" Gibson shouted. "Hi! Prather!" Jennie Prather stopped, turned, and looked at the gesturing Gibson. She shrieked at her husband who scuffled and dragged on the sled, finally halting his dogs.

"The trail is here," Gibson shouted. "Turn the team around."

"This trail is all right," Prather shouted back. "The dogs know more than you do."

"Mrs. Prather, I think you'll find walking much easier on the river," Gibson persisted. "The snow will be very deep in the bush."

"My husband has decided to go this way, Mr. Gibson. It is clearly shorter. I will thank you to keep your opinions to yourself and if you want to take the longer route, feel free." Jennie Prather spoke sharply.

Albert Gibson looked from the defiant woman to the tangle of dogs to the deep soft snow. He shrugged.

"Let's go, then," he said to Bard and they carried on along the river trail, leaving the Prathers to sort out their dog team. By one o'clock Gibson and Bard had arrived at the Hootchikoo roadhouse. After they had eaten, the two men lounged about the bunkhouse waiting for their companions to catch up.

In the meantime, the Prathers started stubbornly up the cutoff. The dogs moved gamely at first but, as the snow became deeper, they began to flounder and thrash. Prather urged and shouted and heaved on the sled but the trail got worse. They worked their way through the deep snow for nearly half an hour although they were making such poor time they had scarcely come a mile. Jennie Prather was becoming angrier with every step. There appeared to be no end to this ridiculous trail and the snow was terribly deep. Her breath was coming in short gasps and she was about to call a halt when, for reasons of their own, the dogs stopped. Mrs. Prather came up to the sled and gratefully leaned on it.

"Well, what now?" she said.

"I'll have to lead them," her husband replied. "The trail is bound to get better."

"What makes you think that? It has got worse and worse; it probably doesn't rejoin the river at all. There is no end in sight." Jennie Prather sniffed loudly.

The trail did not improve. In fact, where, in the beginning, there was a track, if a poor one, there was now almost no trace of travel in the snow. Prather broke trail for his dogs but it was hopeless. After a few hundred yards he stopped.

"We'll turn back," he said, gasping.

"That is the first wise decision you have made today, my love." Jennie Prather was almost winded.

"Thank you, dearest," Prather said, stiffly. "We will go back to the camp, then cut straight down to the river."

"What camp might you be referring to? There is no camp here."

"Yes there is, my precious," said Prather, sarcastically. "If you will be good enough to turn back to the spot where the dogs stopped you will see, back in the bush to your left, a trail which undoubtedly leads to a camp. That is, of course, if you can see past the end of your pointed little nose."

"I can see very well — and I saw no camp."

"I did not say you could see a camp. I said you could see a trail from which you can infer a camp. However, we won't worry about that for when we get to the trail we will not turn left, sweetheart, for that would take us away from the river. Instead, we will go to the right. There is a trail there, too, and we can cut straight over the bank to the ice."

"There is no trail," said Jennie Prather, obstinately.

"There was a trail, dammit. Turn back."

Jennie Prather turned back not, of course, because her husband ordered her to, but because to go ahead was impossible. As she got back to the spot where the dogs had stopped, she saw, with some annoyance, that there was a trail to the left.

"Well, where is the other trail, then?" she asked.

"Right there, my love," said Prather, pointing to the bush on his right. "Don't you see it?"

"All I see is a lot of trees and bush and deep snow — and I have no intention of breaking it."

Prather took a deep breath.

"The river is there — not more than half a mile. Maybe only a few hundred yards. We can catch Gibson."

"I don't care about Gibson. All I know is that the river is back the way we came. I will not go tramping about in the woods because you think you have a short cut. I should never have left Dawson."

"I know. I know. You should never have left Dawson. But if you will just persevere for an hour, we'll get back to the river and on to our meal at Hootchikoo."

"No! I won't do it. I am going back the way we came." And she set off, retracing her steps back to the river trail.

Her husband cursed under his breath. Let her go, he thought. He sat on the sled to catch his breath. Jennie Prather was almost running. The broken snow made walking a little easier and, besides, she was determined that her husband would not be able to claim that they had lost time by not taking his imaginary trail over the bank.

By the time she emerged from the trees and was nearing the

river trail again, she had lost sight of her husband. She slowed a little, head down, to catch her breath. When she looked up, she saw the man, not fifty feet away.

He was standing, not on the river trail, nor on the cutoff, but in the deep snow that lay in the angle between the two trails. He was leaning on a lightly-loaded sled to which was hitched a big, yellow dog. The dog lay in the snow, gnawing patiently at the snow in his foot pads. Jennie Prather looked over her shoulder but her husband and the team had not yet appeared. She turned back to the man.

"You are off the trail," she said. "Are you lost?"

"Not any more," the man replied. "But I got off on that trail yesterday. Just now made my way back."

"Yes, you should have stayed on the river," she said.

"Are you alone?" the man asked.

"No, my husband should be along any minute," she said. She looked back again but her husband had still not emerged from the bush. The man, however, seemed hardly to have heard her and when she turned back, he was working at his dog's paw.

"Is there something wrong with your dog?" she asked.

"Just a little ice. And he's tired." The man bent over his dog again. Jennie Prather walked over to the man's sled.

"He's a beautiful dog," she said.

"Yes'm. He's strong but this new snow has dragged him down."

"What do you call him?"

"Bruce."

"That suits him," she said. "A noble name for a noble animal." She bent over and patted the dog's head. "Is the sled too heavy for you, old fellow?" she said.

"Better not touch him," the man said. Jennie Prather straightened.

"I am a very good judge of dogs, I'll have you know. And I say that dog is very gentle." The man glanced up.

"Better not touch him all the same," he said, as he stood and blew on his hands. "You said your husband was behind you?"

"Yes, he should be along . . . yes, you can hear the dogs now." The team came out of the trees with Prather slogging along in the deep snow, leading. They moved slowly, sometimes on the trail, sometimes in the new snow beside it. It was an open question whether Prather's leading was more hindrance than help because he was clearly winded by the knee-deep snow.

In a matter of minutes he had drawn up on the river trail and stood leaning on the sled, gasping. His dogs yipped perfunctorily at the strange dog, but, getting no response from him, they soon fell silent and flopped on the trail, tongues lolling.

"I am certainly glad we took your shortcut, my love" said Jennie Prather, sweetly. "We are now just as far from Hootchikoo as we were an hour ago. That was splendid work." Her husband looked up, venom in his eye, but he was too winded to speak. Jennie Prather walked back to the trail and stood beside him.

"Now that we have had our constitutional, perhaps we can be on our way." She turned back to the man. "We are on our way to Hootchikoo, Mr. . . . Oh, I am sorry, I have forgotten your name."

"O'Brien. George O'Brien."

"Of course. Are you going our way, Mr. O'Brien? If so, we could travel together." O'Brien looked at the couple, shrugged and turned to his dog.

"There you are, my love," Jennie Prather said to her husband. "With another man along, we might be able to stay on the trail." With that, she turned and walked briskly in the direction of Hootchikoo. Her husband groaned softly, stirred up his dogs and followed. O'Brien trailed behind.

Although it had seemed much longer, the Prathers had only lost an hour ploughing snow in the cutoff. Shortly after two in the afternoon, they arrived at the Hootchikoo roadhouse where they ate and rested. Gibson and Bard were still there, Gibson much refreshed from a nap he had taken after his meal. He determined to set off for Mackay's where he would spend the night. To his surprise, there was no argument from the Prathers who had come in looking somewhat sheepish and more than a little bedraggled. But, upon hearing Gibson's suggestion, they quickly prepared to leave, content for the moment to follow his lead.

A mile out of Hootchikoo, Gibson and his party overtook George O'Brien. The big, yellow dog was ambling along and O'Brien was not pressing him.

"Fine afternoon," said Gibson, as they walked along together. O'Brien nodded.

"I didn't see you at the roadhouse for dinner," Gibson went on.

"Didn't stop."

"Yes, well, travel while the traveling is good, I suppose."

They walked without speaking for a time, the packed snow crunching underfoot.

"Good looking dog you've got there," Gibson said.

"He does the job."

"Is he for sale? I could use a good animal."

"I might sell him."

"How much are you asking?"

"A hundred dollars."

"A hundred dollars?" Gibson exclaimed. "A hundred? Why, I could buy twice the dog in Dawson for half that."

"Then I guess you better buy a Dawson dog," O'Brien retorted. He whistled at the dog and they pulled ahead of Gibson's party.

The Prathers, Ralph Bard, and Albert Gibson arrived at Mackay's in the late afternoon. They had their supper in the dining room and, when they went to the bunkhouse, they found that O'Brien was already there. He had cooked his own meal on the bunkhouse stove — the smell of hot grease was heavy in the air — and was already fast asleep on a lower bunk.

On the morning of 28 December, O'Brien was up early. As he busied himself packing his meager kit, Jennie Prather awoke and stiffly got from her bed, her muscles not fully recovered from the strenuous travel on the cutoff the day before.

"I see we travel together again, Mr. O'Brien," she said.

"Yes."

"Are you coming from Dawson?"

"That's right."

"Oh, when did you leave?"

"About a month ago."

"A month? Whatever have you been doing on the trail all this time?"

"I'm in no hurry. I have just been fooling along."

"I should say you have been. I thought we were making slow enough time but we are fast by comparison with you. Why, at that rate you will be lucky to be in Skagway by next Christmas."

"I'm going to Atlin," O'Brien said.

"Oh! Atlin. That disgusting little town. Why would you want to go there?"

O'Brien peered at the woman from narrowed eyes. He was not certain what to make of her criticism. It was none of her concern where he went, but this was one woman who was accustomed to expressing her views on everything.

"I have friends there," he said cautiously. "But if it doesn't work out, maybe I will go to Nome in the spring."

"Well, Nome does not amount to much either but it is certainly a step up from Atlin."

George O'Brien picked up his gear and left the bunkhouse, relieved to be away from the bothersome woman. And Jennie Prather saw no more of him until they reached Carmack's post that night.

On the night of 29 December, the Prathers arrived at C. D. Camp Number 8. When they walked into the dining room, there, again, was George O'Brien about to sit down at the table with his plate of food. The cook stood, hands on hips, glaring at O'Brien. Then he turned, snatched the frying pan from the stove, and tossed it with a clang on the table in front of O'Brien.

"Here mister, take your gear with you," he said. "I told you to cook on the bunkhouse stove. Nobody cooks on my stove but me."

"I cooked on it," said O'Brien, defiantly.

"I know you did and I told you not to. Cheapskate! You won't buy my meals but you'll happily use my stove."

"And I'll use it again, too, when I get my breakfast."

"You will not. You will use the bunkhouse stove."

"I'll cook on any stove I like. I am paying my way and I won't be pushed by some fool cook. I will see that you are fired. I'll have your job . . ."

"From the look of that mess, you couldn't do my job even if you got it." The cook gestured at O'Brien's meal, fast cooling on the plate.

"I will see you thrown out for treating travelers this way. I'll report you."

"Do that. Go ahead and do that any time you like. And you will find out that the rules are that you can cook on the bunkhouse stove but not on mine. Just like I told you. Cheapskate!"

O'Brien flushed at being called cheap yet again. For a moment it looked as if he might throw his meal at the cook but he glanced at the Prathers, then back at the cook, and finally he sat.

"It has nothing to do with being cheap," he said. "I have better grub than the C. D. Company ever put up, even if I do have to cook it myself."

"Then eat that fine grub of yours. Just stay off my stove." Triumphantly, the cook turned to the newcomers. "Meal for four? Have a seat there and I will be right with you."

On 30 December, the Prathers set out for C. D. Camp Number 6 with O'Brien traveling almost in step.

That same day, Corporal Ryan was patrolling around Minto and he stopped there about midday. In his conversation with John Fussell, he learned that Olsen had, in fact, stayed at Minto Christmas Eve. He had left early on Christmas Day. Where was he going? Nobody was quite certain but, probably, to Five Fingers. Where else would he go? He was stationed at Five Fingers, wasn't he? Did he mention going to Hootchikoo on Christmas Day? Well, no, the Captain couldn't remember anything like that but Mrs. Fussell, after much lip-pursing, allowed as how Olsen must have been going *somewhere* because he had not accepted her invitation to dinner. Then again, perhaps he had mentioned Hootchikoo; it was *so* difficult to recall. The bunkhouse had been full on Christmas Eve and on Christmas Day too. And the *work* one had to do. . . .

Having got very little help, and a miserable meal to boot, Corporal Ryan left for Hootchikoo. As he traveled, he thought of Olsen and how unlike him it was to go back on a promise. Of course, if there was line trouble he would have had to change his plans. But there had been no trouble; the telegraph had been clattering merrily away. So, what had been so urgent that Olsen had to miss Christmas dinner and get back to Five Fingers? And even if there had been some pressing business, Olsen ought to have stopped in later at Hootchikoo with some explanation — he was that sort of man.

The more Ryan thought about the missed Christmas dinner, the less sense it made. By the time he got back to Hootchikoo, he had worked himself into a fine state of bewilderment. That was soon to change.

He had not been at the post for half an hour, when Constable Bacon arrived from Five Fingers.

"Afternoon, Corporal," said Bacon, as he walked into the police post.

"Well, hullo," Ryan said. "You are a long way from home, aren't you?"

"I am and I'm looking for a bed for the night."

"We have a spare bunk that you are welcome to. But what brings you down this way?"

Bacon looked somewhat surprised at the question. "I have been patrolling the ruddy line," he said.

"Then Olsen is here," Ryan said, delighted. "Wait till he comes in here — I have a bone to pick with that man."

"Olsen is not with me."

"Did you leave him behind?"

34

"No. He hasn't been at Five Fingers in the better part of a week." Bacon was clearly annoyed. "That is why I'm having to repair the line by myself."

Ryan felt a chill of apprehension. "Not at Five Fingers?" he exclaimed. "Well, does anyone know where he is, for God's sake? Doesn't Holden know?" This was not a matter of simple rudeness any longer; the lineman was missing, possibly hurt, possibly fallen ill, possibly holed up in a makeshift camp somewhere waiting to freeze.

"We thought he was down this way," Bacon said.

"Well he's not here, and he hasn't been," Ryan snapped. That settles it, he thought. I was right about Olsen all along. He wasn't here on Christmas Day because he was hurt somewhere along the telegraph line. Between here and Minto, too. Probably where the line runs off into the bush and he couldn't make it back to the river. Always happens with one-man patrols.

Ryan walked to the door, yanked it open. "Young!" he shouted. "Young! Come in here." He listened a moment then shut the door again. "Where is that man? When he is not needed, he is forever underfoot."

"What are you doing?" Bacon asked, puzzled by Ryan's outburst.

"Going to hunt for Olsen, of course. Fussell says he is at Five Fingers; you say he was supposed to be here; Holden doesn't know where his own man is. He is out in the bush, that's where he is. And he needs help."

"Corporal, it is dark," Bacon said. "You can't go out now. You could pass within ten feet of him and never see him."

"I could hear him," Ryan said.

"You could — if he was calling. But if nobody on the river has heard him, then he has to be away back in the bush. And you'd never find him at night."

Just then Young came into the post.

"Were you calling for me?" he asked. Ryan turned to him.

"I was. I want the team ready to go ... first thing in the morning," he said.

"To go where?"

"To look for Olsen. He is in the bush between here and Minto. He has a broken leg or something."

"When did that happen?"

"I don't know, Christmas Day, probably."

"You mean he has been down for five days?" Young snorted. "If he has been out there five days, there is no rush. The shape he's in by now, he'll keep till spring."

"We will go at first light," said Ryan, firmly. "Have the team ready."

"Are you walking?" Young asked.

"Yes."

"Then why do you need the team?"

"To haul Olsen back, you clod. Why else?" Ryan was showing exasperation at his dog driver's obstinacy.

"To haul his body back, you mean."

The Corporal fixed Young with an icy stare. "Be that as it may, Mr. Young, I will have the team ready," he said. "What I will not have is further argument from you. Is that clear?"

"Yes, Corporal."

Ryan was up well before first light the next morning, packing for his trip down river to find Olsen. He bundled blankets and the few medical supplies he had. He packed a sack of grub — bread, tea, meat — and, finally, a small flask of medicinal brandy he had carefully squirreled away in his personal kit.

Young was somewhat cranky at being awakened early but, recognizing that Ryan would tolerate no further aggravation, he went about the daily chores and prepared the team to travel. The two men ate breakfast in gloomy silence, washed their dishes, and tidied the cabin. Ryan glanced frequently at the tiny window as if willing the darkness away.

Finally, he said, "There is light enough to see by." And there was too, if you called the pearly gray sky near the horizon daylight.

Young started to comment, then caught himself and walked to the gear piled by the door.

"Is that the lot?" he asked.

"Yes, I think everything is there. You can load and hitch the team and I'll be out directly." Young nodded, pulled on his parka, hoisted Ryan's pack to his shoulder, and left.

Ryan took down his moccasins that were hanging on a peg by the cabin door. He stripped off his felt boots and his socks and, wriggling his toes in the heat from his stove, sorted his footwear for the trail. First, a pair of thin black socks of silk, then two pairs of long woolen socks, long enough to reach his knees. Finally, the moccasins, silvery leather, lacing high on the calf of his leg. He knotted the laces tightly, then rolled the tops of the outer pair of socks down over the knots. Ryan hesitated, weighing a question in his mind. Then he strapped on his service revolver, feeling somehow conspicuous because he rarely wore it. Hardly made sense to wear it under a parka, either, he thought. It would take the best part of a Sunday afternoon to get the thing out if a man ever needed it. Still, he pulled on the parka and his fur hat. He checked the draft on his precious stove, picked up his mitts, blew out the lamp and went out.

The cold struck like the blow from an iron bar, seared his nostrils, and brought tears that froze almost instantly to his lashes. He brushed at them with the back of his mitt, blinked, brushed again. He breathed in short sniffs until the icy air stopped catching in his throat. Ryan stood in the still, crystalline day, reluctant to move, feeling the brutal cold seeping through the soles of his moccasins. For a split-second, he thought selfishly of the delicious warmth behind him in the cabin and was tempted. But he pushed the thought from his mind and with a clumsy, stiff-armed motion, signalled Young to follow. The search for Olsen had begun.

Ryan and Young traveled north on the river trail, walking away from the sunrise. They moved slowly, Ryan methodically searching every patch of bush and hummock of snow along the telegraph line as they proceeded. He was certain that Olsen had patrolled the line on Christmas morning and while the most likely spot for the line man to be stranded unnoticed was several miles downstream, Ryan was determined to cover every foot from Minto to Hootchikoo.

The men had agreed that Young was to keep the team on the packed trail and, where the trail and the telegraph line diverged, Ryan would go on foot to search near the wire. It was slow going and, for Ryan, fiendishly hard work, wading in unbroken snow, now walking easily on the crust, now punching through the crust, knee deep and floundering. He approached with apprehension the first drifts that were big enough to cover a man. He was afraid that when he kicked through one, his feet would strike Olsen's frozen body. But, at the same time, he was afraid he would find nothing at all. And for the first two hours, he found nothing but snow.

It was nearly noon when Ryan and Young reached the point that jutted into the river from their left. The trail on the ice swung in a great arc to the right, weaving through the cluster of islands, and passed around the point. The telegraph line was strung overland, across the thick part of the point. It was here, where the line was over a mile from the river trail, that Olsen would most likely be found. Ryan and Young stopped to catch their breath. Ahead, they could see the rough trail cut in the bush of the point. The trail had not been traveled. This was the trail that Powell's crew had cut early in the winter. They had used the trail but once. However, as such things happen, the ragged cut in the bush became known as Powell's Pork Trail to nearly everyone except William Powell himself.

This same trail was known to Jennie Prather, too. She knew it as her husband's short cut, the one he had so stupidly taken on the way up from Minto, and on which they had finally turned back. The Prathers had seen only the north half of the trail, looking for nothing but a short cut. Ryan and Young, coming from the south, would be looking for the lost lineman.

Ryan pulled off a mitt and, with his bare hand, thawed the ice that almost blocked his nostrils. He snuffled.

"I will go ahead," he said. "I will break trail for the dogs as much as I can. You follow up into the bush a ways and find a spot where there is some good wood. You can rest the dogs and brew some tea. I'll make a loop out to the left and come back along the trail and meet you." Young nodded.

As Ryan started up the trail, he whistled between his teeth, a tuneless mournful whistle that accompanied every exhaled breath. There were clumps of brush that he investigated but, as his eyes scanned the snow ahead, there was no sign whatever of Olsen's having been there. Not that any trail he left would be sharp, of course, because there had been almost a foot of snow since Christmas. But the depression of the tracks ought to be left, softened by the new snow, blurred but not obliterated. There was, however, no sign at all, no fresh cutting where Olsen might have cleared a tree off the line, no footprints, nothing but smooth, unbroken snow.

Ryan plodded on, leaving Young far behind setting up the quick camp. As he got near the spine of the point, the bush became thicker. He had to skirt patches of willow and poplar, then come back to the line to search. Walking became more and more difficult.

Suddenly, he saw in front of him the rumpled snow of a trail. It had been little used and that not recently but it was an indication that another man had been here. Excitement gripped the policeman as he pressed on following the trail. It was probably Olsen's, made as he came down from the north. But, why did he turn back? If he was checking the line, why did he not check it all along the Pork Trail? Because he was hurt, of course, and it must have happened right here somewhere. He turned back because he thought Minto would be easier to reach.

At that moment, Ryan came to the branch in the trail, to the spot at which Prather's dogs had stopped, to the place at which Prather had seen the trail leading back into the bush. Ryan saw that trail too, faint as it was, and he was certain that Olsen had made it. He started down the track and, after walking for several minutes, saw the cabin which Prather had inferred but had not seen. That was it! Olsen was in that cabin.

Ryan's fatigue vanished and he headed for the cabin at a floundering run. But, as he got nearer, hope began to fade. There was a stove pipe but no smoke came from it. And whoever was in the cabin had not been out in a long time; snow was piled smoothly in front of the door. Ryan stopped not ten feet from the cabin, held his breath, listened. The bush was deadly still, deadly cold. The low sun warmed nothing. Not a sound from the cabin. Ryan hesitated to call out as if afraid the brittle world might shatter at his call. He had the sudden urge to draw his revolver but he could not have said why.

For perhaps a quarter of a minute he stood, hoping for some sound, but hearing only his own pulse pounding in his ears. Then he pushed forward, kicked the snow away from the cabin door, and yanked it open. In the icy gloom, he saw a form huddled in the corner but it was not a man. It was a jumbled pile of boxes and sacks of canned food all frozen rock hard. He saw a bunk to the left of the door but it was empty. There was a stove, long cold, some plates and cutlery, a cased rifle hanging from the ridge pole. But Olsen was not there, nor had anyone been there for some time.

It was with mixed relief and disappointment that Ryan began a closer inspection of the cabin — relief that he had not found Olsen dead in the shack and disappointment that what had seemed a lucky lead gave no clue at all about the missing lineman. The policeman dug into the pile of sacks and cartons. There was pilot biscuit, quite a lot of it, too, spilling from the overturned sack. And what's in the cartons? Tinned fruit, by God, all harder than cannon shot, but there must be two or three cases of peaches, counting those in the boxes and the loose cans over by the wall. And the cartons are addressed to Mackay Brothers. The stuff has been hoisted from a cache.

Ryan paused and thought a moment to get his bearings. He reckoned that he was perhaps halfway along the Pork Trail. That meant Mackay's scow would be two miles away, three at most.

There would certainly be no problem for those with sticky fingers, he thought. And it seems they did get into the cache, too. Damn their eyes. And there will be trouble over this for the police at Hootchikoo. You were charged with the responsibility of looking after that cache, weren't you Corporal Ryan? — Yes sir — And yet it was stolen from, wasn't it? — Yes, sir — And it seems the thieves took pretty much what they wanted, when they wanted it? — Yes, sir — Then what was it, Corporal Ryan, that you were doing while this was going on under your very nose?

And so it would go. There would be trouble, no doubt about it. A pox on Mackay's for their meanness, too cheap to hire a guard for the winter. But yet, a lot of stuff is still here. Maybe our thief has not left for good. Corporal Ryan brightened slightly at the thought that the cache thief might still be within reach. Surely he would come back for the food, and for the rifle. Ryan unhooked the rifle case from the straps that bound it to the ridge pole. The case was a rude affair of canvas; the buckle that closed it was broken. Fumbling in his heavy mitts, Ryan drew the rifle from the case. It was not new but appeared to be in fair condition. It was an 1896 Winchester, .40-82 caliber. He worked the lever with his mittened thumb. The action was smooth and free. Whoever owned the weapon knew enough to keep grease out of it in winter when the lubricant stiffened like tar and could lock the action. The rifle was empty. Ryan put it back in the case and hung it from the straps as he had found it. He poked quickly through the remaining equipment, but there was little of interest. He left the cabin, closed the door and headed back along the trail where Young would have camp set up.

When Ryan arrived, Young had tea brewed and some slabs of bread to thaw and toast.

"I thought I was going to have to come looking for you," Young said as he handed Ryan a mug of tea.

"Am I late?" asked Ryan. "Well, yes, I suppose I am. I was snooping around in a cabin up there."

"Olsen wasn't in it, I guess."

"No, he wasn't. I thought certain I had found him. There was an old trail leading back into the bush from the telegraph line — I don't know, a few hundred yards anyway — and at the end there was a cabin. Do you know of any cabin up there?"

Young handed Ryan a piece of bread. "Not that I can recall," he said.

"I don't remember one being there either," Ryan said. "But,

anyway, Olsen wasn't in it. There is a fair stock of Mackay's goods in it, though."

"Stolen, you mean?"

"No doubt about it. There has been nobody around there for at least a week — snow is unbroken — but he may be back because he has left a lot of stuff behind. We will check that cabin regularly for a few days just in case somebody comes to reclaim his property. And I'll get a wire off to Pennycuick. What with all the thefts they have had around Selkirk, I think he should see what we have here."

Young had found the butt of a thin black cigar in an inside pocket. The wrapper was coming loose so he licked it to stick it down.

"What about Olsen?" he asked through a cloud of smoke and frozen breath.

"We go on," said Ryan, shaking the dregs and tea leaves out of his cup into the snow. "I only got about halfway up the cutoff so we will continue until we get back to the river. Then we will search what we can of the river trail on our way to Minto. If we run out of daylight, we will finish the search tomorrow on the way back."

"Right. I will be ready to travel in ten minutes."

"Good. I will meet you up ahead." And Ryan started back along the Pork Trail to search for Olsen.

4
The Tent-Cabin

"Happy twentieth century, Paddy." Pennycuick had arrived at the Hootchikoo post. It was 3 January, 1900. Pennycuick had left Selkirk on New Year's Day after receiving Ryan's wire.

"It is good to see you, Alex," Ryan said. "Did you see the cabin on your way here? Give me your parka and I'll hang it here by the stove."

"Yes, I saw it — Stephens and I were there earlier. We gave the place a thorough going over."

"And?"

"And — not only do you have the cabin of a cache thief, but I know that it is the same pair that we have had to deal with around Selkirk."

"The ones you had the warrant for? asked Ryan, incredulous. "How do you know?"

"A bit of good luck, nothing more," Pennycuick paused, smiling. "The stove," he said. "The stove that is in that cabin on the Pork Trail is the same one I saw in a camp at Hell's Gate. It belongs to our friends Miller and Ross."

"I saw the stove. I would say it looks like any other camp stove."

"Oh no, indeed. Here, let me show you." Pennycuick took out a note book and flipped through the pages. "There. That is a drawing I made of the stove in the cabin. Now just there you can see the damper holes have been punched twice. Mistake the first time, I suppose. But, see how the second punch made a sort of figure eight? That is not usual and that is precisely the way the stove looked in Miller's camp."

"And that puts Miller and Ross on the Pork Trail," Ryan mused.

"No doubt about it, particularly when you consider that there was cutlery and crockery for two in the cabin. However, I am very much interested in when they were there. Now, the trail that you found — that was on the thirty-first?"

"Yes."

"Have you any opinion as to how old the trail was?"

Ryan frowned. "I talked with Young about that. We figured that, because the fresh snow had not been disturbed, the trail was made on the twenty-eighth or before. Of course, it could have been a while before the twenty-eighth, but it was definitely not made after that."

"What about the Pork Trail itself?"

"The same. From the south end, there had been nobody over the trail that I could see traces of. Then about half way along there was an old track that carried right on to the north end. It was covered with new snow, too."

"And you have been watching the place, I gather?"

"Yes, we have; we expected somebody back to get the stuff." Pennycuick wrote the dates in his book and chewed thoughtfully on his pencil.

"It looks as if they are not coming back," he said. "And that is about what we had Miller and Ross pegged for. That is, their past behavior suggested they were simply stealing their way to the outside. So, now we know they were on the Pork Trail around Christmas — that is consistent. But, why, I would like to know, did they leave all that stuff behind?"

"Maybe they stole more than they could carry."

"Possibly. But they had dogs and a sled and from what I saw in their Hell's Gate camp they had very little gear aside from the stove, of course.

"And none of the grub would have to be hauled so very far — just the few miles until they found a roadhouse where they could sell it. And it was good stuff, too. Eminently salable, I would say. Did you take an inventory, by the way?" Ryan shook his head.

"Well, no matter, I have one here." Pennycuick turned a page in his notebook. "Here is what they left. It is most interesting. There were four tins of Eagle Brand milk and the same of Highland cream. Both easy to sell, I would say.

"There was a box of chicken, a box of tinned peaches, tinned cabbage, sausage meat — only a part-case of that but, still . . . All of those things could be sold without difficulty. Now the hardtack may be another matter — perhaps not so many people willing to buy that. But I cannot imagine a roadhouse proprietor who would not jump at the chance to buy milk and fruit.

"Now. Let me see, what else? Oh, yes, there was a ham bone. And I saw a ham in the Hell's Gate camp, not that it means much. There was a bag of .40-82 cartridges and a rifle case. You see, there is another thing: why would anyone leave the case and cartridges behind?"

"Ah. I'm glad you reminded me," Ryan said. "I took the rifle yesterday. That is it in the corner." Pennycuick got up, inspected the rifle, worked the action, eased the hammer down with his thumb.

"Seems to be in working order," he said, as he sat at the table again. "So, it is even more peculiar — a perfectly good rifle is simply left behind."

The two men sat in silence. Pennycuick sketched aimlessly on a blank page of his book. At last, Ryan got up and put a couple of sticks on the fire. The rattle of the stove lid stirred Pennycuick from his thoughts.

"Anyway," he said, "I have sent a wire to Dawson asking that a reminder be sent to all posts on the trail to the effect that Miller and Ross are probably on their way out and that every man ought to have their descriptions." Pennycuick closed his book and tucked it away in his pocket. "Oh, by the way, Paddy," he said, "Did Olsen turn up?"

"No, not a trace."

"They told me in Minto that you had been hunting for him."

"That was how we stumbled on the cabin. Young and I were looking for Olsen and we thought he had been hurt on the Pork Trail."

"Well, I shouldn't be too concerned," Pennycuick said. "There are plenty of places he could be. I have been hearing rumors of a strike on Big Salmon."

"I've heard them, too. But I don't believe Olsen is about to charge off hunting gold, especially in the middle of winter."

"That is not so strange. Nigger Jim Daugherty started a rush last winter, remember?"

"Oh, certainly it could *happen*," Ryan gestured widely. "But the people who follow those rumors are lunatics. You can almost pick them out of a crowd. They look desperate because they came late and have nothing to stake. But Olsen is not that sort of man; he has always been steady."

"Or he could simply have quit and gone outside. He may be in Skagway this very minute."

Ryan shook his head slowly. He had heard all the possibilities from the various people with whom he had spoken about Olsen. He had gone to stake on Big Salmon; he had gone hunting; he had walked away from his job without a word to anyone — all the same ideas arose again and again. But there was never any fact to support them. What Ryan knew to be fact was that Olsen had been at Minto on Christmas morning. And, from there, he had apparently vanished like a wisp of smoke.

"But, if you are intent upon thinking the worst, Paddy, there is a stretch of open water down toward Minto. Olsen may have fallen in. It would be easy enough to do, I suppose." Ryan looked at Pennycuick and nodded sadly.

"I have thought of that, too," he said. "I suspect you have hit it — Olsen is under the ice."

Constable Pennycuick returned to Selkirk on January 5. He and Ryan had gone to the Pork Trail once again and Pennycuick had made a few more sketches of the shack. While they were there, Pennycuick examined the canvas roof of the cabin and found that it had not been made for that purpose but was simply a strip of fabric stretched over a ridge pole, with the sides fastened down to the log walls. The canvas was roughly cut and would, he was sure, prove to have been stolen as well.

With the descriptions of Miller and Ross on the wire, there was nothing more to do but wait and see if they were picked up before they left the territory. Besides, there were other matters to attend to.

When Pennycuick arrived back at Selkirk, there was a message waiting. It came from the police in Dawson and was asking the whereabouts of one Fred Clayson. Inquiries revealed that he had left Dawson for the outside, that he had telegraphed his brother from Selkirk saying to expect him out at Skagway by December 28. Clayson had not arrived and his brother had telegraphed Dawson in an attempt to locate him. Pennycuick stuffed the message into his pocket and went out to see if anyone in Selkirk remembered Fred Clayson.

The most likely places to begin were the lodging houses and, of these, the Selkirk Hotel was probably the best known to travelers. Pennycuick walked across town to the hotel and went in, his arrival announced by the sharp jingles of a set of sleigh bells that hung on the door. A few travelers and regular customers were already in for the day. A game of whist was in progress at a table near the stove and another man sat off by himself, mending a mitt. Einar Trana was sweeping the floor and, between desultory passes with the broom, peering over the shoulder of first one card player then the next. As the bells jangled, Trana looked up. Pennycuick caught his eye and beckoned. Trana took a last glance at the card game and came over to the policeman.

"Constable," he said, nodding his greeting.

"Good afternoon, Mr. Trana," Pennycuick said. "I am looking for Mr. Blake."

"He's not here."

"Well do you know where I might find him?"

"No, I don't. I haven't seen him since — oh, early this morning. He's around town somewhere I suppose but I don't know where."

"It is no matter; you can probably help me. I am looking for a man named Clayson. Do you know the name?"

"Clayson?" Einar Trana looked, squinting, over Pennycuick's left shoulder, as if expecting an answer posted on the wall. "Let me think now," he said. "Clayson, you say. No, I don't think I recognize the name. I knew a Clayburn once, but he was in Seattle. That wouldn't be him."

"Probably not."

"What did this Clayson do, anyway?"

"Nothing, as far as I know. We are just trying to locate him."

"There's a woman after him, I suppose." Trana looked hopeful that a good story was in the offing.

"I really could not say," Pennycuick replied. "But since you do not remember him, perhaps I could see the register. That would tell me if he stayed here."

"Oh, no, I don't think I could do that . . . Mr. Blake wouldn't want me . . ." Pennycuick raised his hand, stopping the protest.

"There will be no problem, I assure you. If Mr. Blake has any questions, simply have him see me about it. You will be betraying no confidences. Please, Mr. Trana, the register?" Trana walked reluctantly behind the desk. He took the leather-bound book from a bottom shelf and laid it on the bare plank surface. He was clearly unhappy at the prospect of the police probing about in the hotel's business.

"I'm not sure I ought to let you have this," he said. Pennycuick smiled and gently lifted Trana's hand off the register.

"I will only be a moment," he said and began flipping through the pages. "Perhaps the night of the twenty-first," he muttered, running his finger down a page. "Yes, here we are: F. Clayson."

"Let me see that," said Trana, turning the book. "Where is it? Oh, yes, I've got it. All right, now, who else was here that day?

Maybe I can place him." He studied the page a second, then stabbed at it with his forefinger. "There! Relfe. I know him. Well, I don't really know him but I remember him. See, there's other names between his and Clayson's but they were traveling together. I remember him now." Trana chuckled, embarrassed. "I ought to remember Clayson — I busted his cycle."

Pennycuick showed mild surprise. "He was traveling by wheel?" he asked.

"Yup. I remember it now plain as day. There was five or six people all at the hotel at once. And I remember Relfe because I was talking to him later in the evening — we knew some of the same people, you see. Anyway, after they all got signed in and whatnot, I was doing some choring around and I spied this cycle propped against the wall outside. I thought I might buy it, you see, when I found out who owned it, but, in the meantime, I'd just take a ride to test it. Well, I jumped on and damn if I didn't bust the pedal right off it. When I looked close, I saw that it had been busted before, and repaired but not very solid. Well a cycle with one pedal is not much use — you can't ride like this . . ." Trana lurched out from behind the desk, stamping his right foot. It was a passable imitation of a man on a bicycle with only one pedal, Pennycuick thought. He smiled and nodded at Trana to continue.

"So anyways," Trana went on, "I checked on who owned the cycle. It turned out to be Clayson — I didn't remember the name, you see, but I remembered the cycle. Well, he was pretty good about it. Didn't seem to bother him much. But he asked if there was anybody around town who could fix the pedal."

"And did you get it repaired?"

"Not really well. We went over to the sawmill and saw Charlie Dorman. He's pretty handy, you know. Well, he tried to fix it but it was no good — as soon as we tried the cycle, we could see that the pedal would never hold.

"So Clayson says he's in merchandise and, if I buy the cycle, he'll send me a new pedal from the outside. But I didn't bite on a deal like that. I didn't say it to him, mind, but how could I be sure he'd send the pedal?"

"Quite right, Mr. Trana. So, I take it you did not buy the wheel?"

"Right."

"What became of it? Do you know?"

"Clayson took it with him. The two of them left the next

morning for upriver and he was pushing the cycle."

"And you are certain that Relfe was with him?"

"Oh, yeah. They were traveling together — had done all the way from Dawson."

"This Relfe chap, you said you knew him . . .?"

"No, not really, just that we knew some of the same people."

"Yes, I'm sorry," Pennycuick said. "Do you know his first name?"

"Lynn, I think."

"How is it spelled?"

"Oh, Lord, I don't know. L-i-n, L-i-n-n-, L-y-n. Something like that." Pennycuick made a quick entry in his notebook.

"Have you seen the man since?" he asked. Trana promptly shook his head.

"No, they were heading out. Probably never be back."

"All right. Thank you Mr. Trana. And if there is any trouble with Mr. Blake about the register, tell him to see me."

"No trouble, Constable," said Trana, returning the register to its shelf.

Pennycuick turned and left the hotel, his departure, as his arrival, announced by the clash of sleigh bells.

He immediately went to the sawmill where he found Charles Dorman. The story, Pennycuick was sure, would be no different — Dorman would simply corroborate what Trana had already told him. The interview would take about ten minutes and that would be the end of the whole affair, save for sending the information to Dawson. Of course, there was something unforseen: the fact that Clayson had been traveling with Relfe. Dawson could have found that, if they had tried, but no doubt the lazy sods had passed the message on to Selkirk, having made no enquiries of their own. It would be just like them.

The interview went as predicted. Yes, Dorman remembered the bicycle and, yes, he remembered the owner. Einar brought the bicycle over to have the crank fixed. No, the repair was not a proper one — it needed new parts. No, Dorman could not recall the date exactly but it was sometime before Christmas.

Pennycuick made brief notes, mainly to the effect that Trana and Dorman were agreed. Then, as he was about to leave, Pennycuick asked, "Did you ever see Clayson or Relfe after you tried to fix the wheel?"

"I did." Dorman carved a piece of a plug of tobacco with his pocket knife, popped the chew in his mouth, and gnawed thought-fully.

"You saw them again, you say," Pennycuick prompted.

"Yessir, I did and Clayson was still pushing that fool bicycle, too."

"Where was that?"

"At Minto. Well, actually, I saw them twice, you might say. Once on the trail below Minto and then again at the roadhouse."

"And when was that?"

"Christmas Eve."

"How did you happen to be at Minto?"

"I was helping build a trail through the bad ice this side of Minto. For the horses hauling freight, that is. And during the day, I saw Clayson and Relfe on the trail. I gave them a wave. Then I saw them again at the roadhouse that night."

"But, if you saw them here on the twenty-second, or thereabouts, how were you ahead of them up the river?" Dorman shrugged.

"I don't rightly know," he said. "Left before them, I imagine. We weren't much ahead of them anyway because we only had — oh — maybe a good half-day's work to do on that trail. There was just the one bad spot, really."

"All right. Then you saw them at the roadhouse."

"Yes. That evening."

"Did either of them say where they were going at that time?"

"Well, Skagway, of course. They were heading out."

"But did they actually say that or could they have been going somewhere else?"

"Oh, no, they were going out. I talked with Clayson a bit in the bunkhouse. He's a merchant, you know, and he said he had to be out to help his brother."

"Was there anything else said in the bunkhouse?" Pennycuick asked. Dorman shifted his quid, spit on the dirt floor of the shop, and thought a moment.

"Don't think so," he said. "It was just the usual bunkhouse chat. Fussell's hired man and one of the constables were passing a bottle of whiskey, I know, them and another fellow — the lineman — what's his name?"

"Olsen?"

"That's him. They were passing a bottle, like I said. They weren't rowdy or anything."

"That was your last contact with Clayson and Relfe, then?"

"Yes. Well, I saw them as they left the next morning, of course. They were away before me on Christmas Day but I saw them leave."

"Heading upstream, were they?"

"Right. Them and the lineman. And Clayson was still trundling his bicycle." Dorman chuckled at the thought of the fool man pushing a useless bicycle but Pennycuick was not amused. It was as if a tiny alarm bell had sounded in his brain as he suddenly made the connection between Clayson and the missing lineman.

"Olsen was with them, you say?" he asked, calmly.

"He was."

"I thank you, Mr. Dorman. You have been a great help."

Pennycuick walked slowly back to the Police post, mulling over his new-found facts. Don't we have a fine pickle now, he thought. Now we have three men leaving Minto. One does not arrive at Hootchikoo, the second does not arrive at Skagway, and who knows about the third.

How could Ryan have missed the fact that Olsen was not alone when he left Minto? He said he had talked to the people at the roadhouse. But, then, perhaps it is not surprising, either. Olsen was a regular customer at the roadhouse; nobody knew the other two. And what with the dozens of people coming and going at the roadhouse, the proprietor would probably take no notice even if he had seen the three leaving together. But, all that aside, they surely are placed together by Dorman's story. And what to make of it?

It did not strain belief to imagine Olsen, traveling alone, punching through a bit of thin ice and, being unable to haul himself out, drowning and being drawn under the ice. But to imagine a party of three doing it was quite another matter. Even if they were all blind drunk they could not possibly troop, one after the other, into that big open stretch above Minto. Utterly impossible. And if the lead man broke through somewhere, would the other two fall in on top of him? Ridiculous.

And while Olsen could have gone hunting, as some said, that idea was now much less likely, too. Clayson was a merchant and, probably not given to spontaneous hunting trips or to mad scrambles to stake on some creek, either. He had business commitments. So, what had become of him?

Was Clayson carrying money, perhaps, or gold? Anyone selling goods in Dawson was likely to have a fair bit of both and, if he was foolish enough to carry it on him, someone may have been tempted to rob him. Olsen? Doubtful, if Ryan was right about him. But what about this other fellow, this Relfe? He had been traveling with Clayson; possibly he knew of any money he was carrying. Relfe could have robbed his companion and vanished outside. Yes, that was possible, especially in view of the fact that, so far, Relfe had not been reported missing.

But, no, robbery explains nothing. Even if there was a robbery, one still must explain the men's disappearance. And that suggests Clayson was killed during the robbery and his body disposed of. But, what about Olsen? If Relfe planned to rob his partner, he must have had plenty of chances to do it when there was nobody within five miles. Why would he choose to do it when the lineman was around to complicate matters? Unless Olsen helped him.

And Clayson's body — if he was, in fact, killed — where was it? Ryan searched the entire trail and found nothing. So, if there is a body, it is either deep in the bush or under the ice.

Oh, yes, a splendid pickle: two men gone without trace. And if there was a robbery, and if there was a murder, and if Relfe did it, he was long gone.

Pennycuick wired his information to Dawson — that is, three men had left Minto on 25 December, Olsen was missing as well as Clayson and enquiries ought to be made as to Relfe's whereabouts.

As an afterthought, he added a reminder that Miller and Ross, suspected cache thieves, had not yet been located. For the first time, he noted that the men had two dogs — one black and the other a yellow and white Newfoundland.

5

O'Brien Arrested

When a traveler reached Tagish, he knew he was nearly out — in a day or so he would reach the passes and, then, Skagway. Tagish was, very much, a place to pass through, as thousands did on their way to Dawson. The permanent residents of Tagish were Indians and Mounted Policemen and few others.

Because of the sort of town Tagish was, the policemen were attuned to travelers and, in addition to their other duties, paid close attention to those who came and went. Mostly, they were concerned with gold-hunters heading into the Yukon, concerned with the kind and quantity of gear the travelers carried. The stories of hardship and starvation from '97 and '98 had done little to ensure that late-comers would be properly equipped. Even yet, men could be found at Tagish, heading for Dawson, with enough grub for one light lunch, no money, no decent boots or caps or mitts. These men were intercepted and given a terse lesson in survival. It was the main job of the police.

By January 7, the Tagish Post had received the wire from Dawson describing Miller and Ross. George Graham, Staff Sergeant, NWMP, had read the wire as it came in and had snorted with disgust. Now, what was a fellow supposed to do with a message like this? Look at those descriptions! Hell's afire, three-quarters of the people in the Yukon are of middling height and middling complexion. And fully half of *them* have dark hair. Possibly unshaven? That excludes women — or most of them. Ridiculous waste of time sending messages like this. Surely policemen ought to know better. Graham filed the wire on a spike and went out to patrol the town.

It was a bleak, cloudy day, cold and perfectly still. The silence was broken only by Graham's footsteps crunching in the packed snow. As he walked he checked, almost unconsciously, the hundred small signs that might mean trouble. But, all was well; comforting plumes of smoke issued from the chimneys of cabins scattered here and there along the trail. Midday, of course, was a fine time to check on the town because travelers would be stopping to eat and one needed only to wander into the roadhouses to see who was traveling. This was what Graham did and satisfied himself that nothing was amiss.

As he returned to the post, however, he spotted a strange team of horses tied outside the barracks bunkhouse. They seemed a bedraggled pair and, as Graham got closer, he realized that one of the horses was wet. It had obviously gone through the ice and was in bad condition. He walked up to the wretched animal and touched its shoulder. There was a soft crackle under his mitt as he stroked down the horse's side to its rump. The hair was frozen stiff and, in due course, the horse would be, too.

"Whoa, there, steady," Graham said, gently, slapping the horse's rump as he walked back to the bobsled it was hitched to. The sled was caked with ice as was the dogsled and camp gear that were loaded on it. Graham walked slowly around the bobsled, checking, until his eye was caught by an ice-encrusted robe packed near the front. He smashed some of the ice and partly unfolded the robe. Buffalo robe — government issue. But this was no government rig. Answers were in order.

As Graham went to the bunkhouse door, a yellow and white dog got up from beside the path and wagged its tail tentatively. Graham patted the dog's head as he passed and went into the bunkhouse. Inside, a lone man stood near the stove, his back to the door. His outer clothing was hung around the stove drying. The man stood in his stocking feet, suspenders looped at his sides, trousers steaming in the heat from the stove. He wrung a trickle of water from a pair of knitted mitts.

"Good day to you," said Graham. The man turned and stared levelly at the policeman.

"Afternoon. I was just warming here. There was nobody around . . ."

"Fine. Fine. You are welcome to use the place." The man nodded his thanks and turned back to the stove, shaking a fine spray from the mitts. The droplets hissed and popped as they struck the hot iron.

"Do you own the blacks out front?" Graham asked.

"Yeah."

"Well, you'd better get them stabled or you are going to lose the gelding. He looks in pretty poor shape."

"Where is there a stable I can use?"

"There is an empty stall in ours across the way. Use that."

"Thanks. I'll put them away as soon as I get dry."

"We won't wait. I will get one of the men to do it right away." Graham left the bunkhouse.

He returned in about five minutes. "It is taken care of," he said.

"Thanks," said the man.

"Now," said Graham, "You can tell me two things — your name and how it happens that you have a Police robe on your sleigh." The man exhaled a long, slow sigh then looked at Graham.

"My name is George O'Brien," he said, quietly. "And the robe was given to me in Dawson."

"Who gave it to you?"

"The Police."

"I see," Graham said. But his eyebrows were raised in total disbelief.

"Yeah. I was on the woodpile last summer and when the police let me go, they found they had lost my robe — a good one it was, too. So, they gave me that one as a replacement."

"When were you released"

"I'm not sure — in the summer."

"Come now, every convict knows the date of his release. Anyway, I want to know because your story will have to be checked. And unless I get the word from Dawson about the robe, you, sir, will be our guest."

"I tell you I don't remember the date. It would be September, sometime, but I don't remember exactly."

"Very well. I am going to enquire about you, Mr. O'Brien. In the meantime, you stay put. The men will be watching for you so don't try to leave." O'Brien said nothing but turned back to his clothes, shifting some away from the heat, moving others closer.

"You hear me?" Graham asked.

"I hear you," O'Brien said, not looking up.

George Graham sent a wire to Dawson asking about O'Brien. The description he sent was a full one, including a description of the black team, the bobsled, and the yellow and white dog. The wire was a long one and, when it arrived in Dawson, it caused some amusement among the policemen there — Graham was at it again. He was forever thumping a drum about proper descriptions and one that ran on as this one did could have been sent by nobody else.

All that was needed, of course, was the man's name: George O'Brien. It was checked against the jail record and confirmed. The same name was found in the records of the Provost Sergeant. All the dates corresponded, roughly.

By three o'clock in the afternoon, Graham had his reply. O'Brien had told a straight story; his robe had been lost and later replaced with one of government issue. He had been released on September 16, after serving six months for breaking jail. Graham looked at the message scornfully. It was of little value to know the man had broken jail. It may have been useful to know why he was in jail in the first place, but there was no mention of that. However, there was no reason to hold O'Brien now and Graham went to the bunkhouse to tell him.

Surprisingly, O'Brien did not appear relieved that the wire had confirmed his story. When Graham told him the news, he shrugged and asked if his team could stay overnight in the police stable because he would not be leaving until morning. Graham agreed and O'Brien left the bunkhouse without another word. Strange fellow, thought Graham. Quiet, not sullen exactly but certainly quiet. But then a tour on the woodpile — two tours, actually — would be more than enough to get him known to the police in Dawson. He would scarcely have been able to walk down the street, but he would be watched to make sure he did not spit on the sidewalk. That kind of attention would make most men sullen. Anyway, it looks as if the Yukon has lost its shine for Mr. O'Brien. He will not likely be back.

At that moment, in Dawson, there was much hooting and laughter as several policemen with nothing better to do passed Graham's telegram around and gleefully dissected it. Some of them had heard, at first hand, Graham's views on the notes a policeman ought to take, on the detailed descriptions of people and places that, he believed, ought to be recorded. They swapped stories about Graham, each yarn better than the next. Those who did not know Graham and who had no stories to tell, were not to be left out of the merriment, however. So, they commented loudly about the dreadful waste of wire time sending useless information about horses, dogs, and gear.

In the midst of the general hilarity, however, a note was struck. Nobody would be able to recall later just who had made the connection but a link was made between Graham's wire and an earlier one from Selkirk. And the point that registered was the big yellow and white dog. The Selkirk wire had called him a yellow and white Newfoundland, Graham's merely a big yellow and white sled dog. When this common factor was first mentioned, it, too, was treated lightly. Someone said Graham ought to be reprimanded for missing the breed; someone else asked how an Englishman like

Pennycuick would know a Newfoundland dog anyway. But, the connection had been made and it nagged like a chipped tooth.

At last, Pennycuick's message was located and compared with Graham's. The discrepancies were several. Pennycuick was after two men; Graham had only one. Graham's man had a team of black horses; Pennycuick's men did not. The names in Pennycuick's wire were Miller and Ross. Graham's man was George O'Brien and that name had been checked in the records. The descriptions of the men tallied, however, and there was the big yellow dog. If, in the jostling hordes, all men came to be more or less featureless, a dog did not. A dog, and a horse, too, for that matter, might stick in one's mind when the owner would be promptly forgotten. And how many yellow and white Newfoundlands were there anyway?

By five o'clock that afternoon, a second wire was sent from Dawson to Tagish. This one instructed Graham to hold the man O'Brien on suspicion of cache theft. When he received the message, Graham permitted himself a smile of self-satisfaction. At least somebody in Dawson was alert enough to get things done — even if they were late. And Graham was pleased with himself, too, because his ceaseless observation was bearing fruit: he knew exactly where to find George O'Brien. Graham had not been snooping on the man, precisely, merely staying aware of what was happening in Tagish. Graham learned that, in the few hours since his release, O'Brien had taken a shine to Jennie Murphy. The story was that he had met the lady in the afternoon and claimed to be an old acquaintance from Dawson. Jennie had denied it, apparently, but O'Brien had insisted and pressed upon her the use of his dog to transport her back to her house. The lady had accepted the offer and, in due course, O'Brien had headed off to retrieve his dog and sled. So, when Constable Dixon returned from Skagway that evening, Graham knew exactly where to send him to arrest George O'Brien.

If Tom Dixon was annoyed at the prospect of hiking to the Indian houses after a day on the trail, he did not let it show. He listened to the detailed instructions from Graham, including the minute description of O'Brien, then he nodded.

"I will be able to catch someone in the bunkhouse," he said. "Duncan should be around. I'll get him to come along. We will be back in an hour and a half."

Dixon left the guardroom and crossed to the bunkhouse where he found Constables Joyce and Duncan. Both men were sitting near the stove, Joyce dozing, Duncan writing a letter.

"Who wants to take a walk to Dawson Jennie's," Dixon asked. Duncan looked up eagerly.

"Count me in. Yes, sir, you can count me in," he said, hurriedly folding his paper and tucking it away.

"Not for a party," Dixon said. "There's supposed to be a fellow there that Staff Graham wants arrested."

"Oh," Duncan said, subdued. "It's work. All right, Tom, I'll give you a hand." Joyce stretched and yawned.

"I may as well come for the walk, too," he said, following Duncan to the coathooks.

"What did this fellow do" Duncan asked.

"He's a thief, apparently. And an ex-convict. Seems he was helping himself to cached goods somewhere around Selkirk."

"Has he got a weapon?"

"Graham didn't think so. The fellow's gear is still in the stable — and his rifle is with the rest of the stuff." Dixon paused a second. "But," he went on, "to be on the safe side, you better lug a rifle along. If we don't need it, I'll carry it back." Duncan picked up a rifle and his mitts.

"Go ahead. I will take care of the lantern," Joyce said. He checked the stove and blew out the lantern, plunging the bunkhouse into darkness.

The sky had remained overcast and, as the three policemen started out, it was several minutes before their eyes became accustomed to the inky blackness. But, once away from the lamp light streaming from the windows at the post, they were soon able to see the trail, faintly outlined in deep purple, as if the snow itself were weakly phosphorescent. They walked swiftly, Dixon and Duncan abreast, Duncan with the rifle cradled in the crook of his arm. Joyce trailed several yards behind. It was nearly two miles from the post to the Tagish houses, a scattering of cabins of which Jennie Murphy's was the first they would reach. The trip took just over half an hour and, as the policemen rounded the last sharp bend, they could see lights glowing in cabins here and there. Two hundred yards ahead, in the middle of the cluster, was the roadhouse run by Tagish Charlie. Lanterns were hung on either side of his door, spilling warm, inviting light on the snow. The policemen stopped but their approach had been detected by the village dogs — of which there were several score — which set up a most unholy din, barking and howling and yanking on their tether chains.

"Which cabin is Jennie's?" Joyce asked. "I can't tell them apart in the dark."

"That one, the first one with a light. There . . . now what the hell! Somebody put the light out." Dixon sniffed. "You don't suppose that O'Brien fellow is waiting inside for us, do you? In the dark? Beside the door?"

"With a pick handle?" Duncan added.

"Yeah, or a pistol," said Dixon. "Now, listen. Jennie doesn't speak English, does she?"

"I hear she can say 'twenty dollars' real clear," said Joyce, elbowing Duncan who snorted with smothered laughter.

"Here, now. Shush," said Dixon. "They can probably hear us."

"Not likely," said Joyce. "They couldn't hear a brass band above those damn dogs."

"All right," said Dixon. "Here's what we will do. You two stay here and watch the cabin. Make sure nobody slips out. I'll go to Charlie's and get one of the boys to interpret for me. That way we can talk to Jennie without O'Brien knowing what is going on." With that, Dixon left for Charlie's, a hundred yards further down the trail. As he moved out of earshot, Joyce muttered out of the corner of his mouth.

"Good plan, Tom," he said. "If a woman called Murphy is an Indian, what do you suppose a man called O'Brien is?" And he and Duncan collapsed in mirth, giggling and snuffling like little boys in church.

In a matter of minutes, Dixon was back with Patsy Smith in tow.

"Anything happen?" Dixon asked.

"Not a thing," said Joyce.

"Right. Now, Patsy, that's Jennie's cabin, isn't it?"

"Yup."

"Good. You talk to her in Indian and tell her who is here."

"Huh?"

"I say, tell her, in Indian, who is here."

"Yup." Patsy spoke briefly in his own language. There was a pause, then a faint reply from the cabin, a reply that was nearly lost in the dogs' yapping.

"She says: Jennie and her friends."

"What sense does that make?" Dixon asked. Then realization dawned. "Oh, hell, Patsy, I said tell her who is here, not ask her who is there." Joyce and Duncan were struck by another fit of giggling.

"Listen, Patsy. Say 'Tom Dixon is here. The police are here.' Tell her to light the lamp."

"Yup." Patsy spoke again. Dixon heard his own name in the unintelligible throat sounds. Maybe that meant the message was right this time. They waited for perhaps a long count of ten, then a match flared and a thin light could be seen at the window.

"Now, say we are coming in," said Dixon, as he moved toward the cabin. Duncan, with the rifle, was a step behind and to the right. Dixon moved quickly, shoved the door open hard, fully expecting it to bump against the man poised behind it. But the door swung fully open, banging against the wall. From the doorway, Dixon could see Jennie standing near the back wall and three other girls sitting, wide-eyed, on a bench beside the stove. The candle flame flickered and leaped in the draft from the open door. In the weak yellow wash, Dixon could also see two men. The one sitting on the bunk, rolling a cigarette, was a policeman. Dixon knew him well, and ignored him.

The dark man sitting behind the stove had to be O'Brien. Dixon crossed the cabin with Duncan close behind. The rifle was still in the crook of Duncan's arm but his mitts were off, swinging from a cord over his neck. Dixon spoke to the man in the shadows.

"Is your name O'Brien?" he asked.

"That's right."

"Good enough." Dixon paused, unconsciously dropping the pitch of his voice slightly, adopting his official tone.

"George O'Brien," he said, "I arrest you in the name of Her Majesty, the Queen." There was silence. Even the dogs had ceased their racket. Then, softly, Jennie Murphy crossed behind the police men and closed the cabin door. O'Brien sat, his eyes flicking from Dixon to Joyce to Duncan to the rifle, back to Dixon.

"Still fretting about your robe, are you?" he said.

"You will find out all about it at the post. Now come along." O'Brien got up slowly.

"You get proper tedious, you know that?" he said. "I told your man I was issued that robe and so I was." Dixon stepped directly in front of O'Brien.

"Never mind, I said. You'll find out soon enough. Come along." Dixon seized O'Brien by the shoulder and began to propel him toward the door. O'Brien shook the hand off.

"Don't push — I'll come. But I want my coat."

"Get it, then," Dixon snapped.

"And my dog and sled are outside."

"All right. All right. Just be quick about it," Dixon said, stepping aside to let O'Brien pass. Jennie Murphy said something to O'Brien that Dixon did not catch. O'Brien grinned and winked at her as he picked up his coat.

Forty-five minutes later, Constable Dixon and his party arrived at the Tagish post guardroom. Staff Sergeant Graham was waiting for them.

"Mr. O'Brien," Graham said. "We meet again."

"I told you the robe is mine," O'Brien said, resignedly. "How many times do you have to be told?"

"Oh, the robe is yours all right," Graham said, smiling. "But some of our people down river want to talk to you about some caches."

"Caches?" said O'Brien, clearly startled.

"Yes. It seems somebody has been stealing from frozen-in scows and we think it was you. You can help us if you are willing to tell us what you know about the thefts."

"I know nothing about it," said O'Brien.

"That is what I thought," Graham answered. He turned to Dixon. "You men call it a day; we will handle him now." Dixon nodded and turned to leave, nearly bumping into Inspector Wood who had just entered the guardroom.

"Sir!" snapped Dixon, stiffening.

"Carry on, men, carry on," said Wood. "You have our man, I see. Good work, Constable Dixon. Have you had anything to eat?"

"No, sir."

"I figured as much. Get on over to the roadhouse and get a meal. You can't work all day in this cold without some food in your belly."

"Yes, sir," said Dixon. Wood nodded a curt dismissal and Dixon left. Wood turned to Graham.

"Search him thoroughly, Staff. I will be grateful for a copy of your inventory when you have it complete."

"We will get right at it, sir."

"Good." As Inspector Wood left the guardroom, Graham turned to O'Brien.

"Over here and empty your pockets on the table," he said. The man stood, coat open, staring steadily at the policeman. He made no move to obey. "Come on, man. Strip them off," Graham said. "Let us not get started on the wrong foot. You will be with us for a while."

Graham turned to Routledge. "If you will be good enough to write them down, sir," he said, "I will dictate the prisoner's effects to you as I search." Routledge nodded and drew several sheets of paper from the desk.

"We will start with his other gear," Graham said. "At the rate he is moving, it will be ten minutes before he has his clothes off and his pockets emptied. So . . . one black gelding." Routledge began to write.

"One black mare. One pair light bobsleds. One dog sled. Two pairs of single harness. Now, just a moment. There is breeching missing from one set. Make that two pairs of single harness, incomplete." Routledge nodded, scribbled, Graham went on.

"Two horse blankets, worn — so badly worn as to be worthless, I'd say. No, I am sorry, sir, don't put that down — just say, horse blankets, worn. Right, where was I? Oh yes, one train dog, yellow and white. That takes care of the stuff outside, I think." Graham walked across to O'Brien's gear that had been brought into the guardroom and piled in a loose jumble near the door. "Now for this stuff," he said. "One map of Alaska." He paused and glared sharply at O'Brien.

"You are not making much headway, Mr. O'Brien," he said. "When I get to wanting to search your pockets, I will not be kept waiting."

Graham plucked two undershirts from the pile of goods on the floor. "Two undershirts," he said. "One yellow and one gray." With the map and the shirts, he began a second pile in a clear space on the floor.

"One set of gold scales, with case. Two Colt's revolvers, both .41 calibre, numbered . . . let's see . . . 766 and . . . 223." Graham examined both revolvers, confirming that they were empty. "And there are two cowhide holsters, one with a belt." He put the revolvers in the holsters and dropped the lot on the undershirts.

"One Yukon map, Anderson's. One pair of field glasses, with case. Three pairs of socks, woolen, black. One pair of mitts, woolen. Now there are cartridges here, sir, some Winchester 30s and some .41 revolver rounds. Give me a minute to count them."

True to his habit, Graham counted them twice, mumbling to himself as he sorted through the handful of dull brass.

"There are thirty rounds of Winchester center fire 30s and thirty-two rounds, revolver, .41 caliber, fitting the two Colts — no, hold it, sir, don't write that." Graham realized that his inventory could well become evidence in court and, knowing what he did of the blindly literal mental processes of most lawyers, he imagined a court scene in which he would be questioned about his search.

"And you found .41 caliber revolver shells, you say, Staff Sergeant?"

"Yes, sir."

"And those rounds fitted the revolvers, I believe you said?"

"Yes, sir."

"No doubt you tried the cartridges in the revolvers to see if they did, in fact, fit."

"No, sir."

"No? You did not put the cartridges in the cylinders?"

"No, sir."

"Is it a difficult task for a policeman to put cartridges in a revolver?"

"No, sir."

"In fact, it is a very easy thing to do, isn't it, Staff Sergeant?"

"Yes, sir."

"But you didn't do it."

"I did not."

"So, you do not know — of your own knowledge — that those cartridges actually fit the Colt's revolvers, do you?"

And on it would go. It was a small point, almost trifling, to the layman's mind. But Graham knew that such small details often figure large in court and it was the clever policeman who anticipated the details and answered the questions beforehand. Make sure the murder weapon will actually fire, check that the witness is not color blind, open the horse's mouth and look at his teeth, yourself.

Graham unholstered the revolvers, slipped two of the .41 caliber rounds in each and worked the action, trapping the hammer with his thumb so as not to blow holes in the guardroom floor.

"Right," he said, unloading the revolvers, "Now write thirty-two rounds, revolver, .41 caliber, fitting the two Colts." He rummaged in the pile of gear once again.

"Needles and thread. One razor, Wade and Butcher, with case. One shaving brush. One ball of wool, black. One looking glass, broken." Graham dumped the toilet articles back in the drawstring bag in which he found them. "One curry comb. One miner's pick. Looks like it has had precious little use, Mr. O'Brien.

"Dog harness. Did I not list that earlier, sir, just after the dog?" Routledge ran his forefinger up the written list.

"No. It is not here," he said.

"Hm," said Graham, obviously annoyed with himself. "I thought I had all the outside stuff listed. Someone must have brought the dog harness in just now."

"I believe Constable Joyce did," said Routledge.

"Well, good for him. Right, I will carry on, then. One set of dog harness. One Indian buffalo robe, police issue. Two driving bitts. One Winchester carbine, .30-30." Graham slipped the rifle out of its case. "No serial number. No — hold it, sir. Change that to: number filed off." Then Graham hunted through the pile of listed goods, produced the rifle cartridges and satisfied himself that they fitted the Winchester. "One carbine cover, canvas with leather fittings," he said, as he put the rifle back in the case and set it aside.

"That takes care of that lot. Now, Mr. O'Brien, your personal effects. Here now! Change into the clothes on the chair there and be quick about it. Those clothes are quite clean." Graham went to the table. "All right, now for the pocket stuff. Two pieces of lead pencil. One pocket knife, two blades. Part of a package of cigarette papers. And what is this?" He unfolded a heavily creased slip of paper. "It is a receipt," he said. "It is for two hundred dollars for . . . let me see . . . horse, harness and, what is this . . . oh, bobsled. Of course, yes. It says: two hundred dollars, cash received in full. And it is signed. It looks like H. C. Schock. I suppose that must be Schock from the roadhouse down at Laberge. Is that right? O'Brien! I am talking to you!" O'Brien stared sullenly at the policeman but said nothing.

"Have it your way," Graham said, shrugging. "We will find out in our own time." He set the receipt aside. "Now there is one cartridge, Winchester center fire, .30-30 caliber. One gold dust bag, empty."

"There is money now, sir. I will count it carefully; I do not want any mix-up with the prisoner's money." Graham counted the bills once, then again more slowly.

"We have sixty dollars and fifty cents in total. The denominations are as follows. One twenty dollar bill, Bank of Commerce, No. 24128. One ten dollar bill, Bank of British Columbia, No. 24950. One ten dollar bill, U.S. silver No. E15016627. One ten dollar bill, U.S. National Currency, No.R490874. One ten dollar bill, Bank of British North America, No.135764. And one fifty cent piece, U.S. silver."

Graham paused, surveying the litter of O'Brien's effects. "I believe that is everything, sir. If you would like to go, I will take the list and, when Mr. O'Brien is out of his clothes, I will add them to the rest. Oh, and if you see the Provost, sir, you might tell him he can get the list from me so he can make the entries in the Prisoner's Effects Book."

It took but a few more minutes for O'Brien to dress in the clothes supplied him. It was an odd assortment but, as Graham had promised, the clothes were clean and a surprisingly good fit, if one ignored the trousers which ended fully five inches above the ankle. O'Brien sat, eyes fixed glumly on the wall opposite. Graham gathered the clothes which O'Brien had dropped and set them on the table.

"All right, O'Brien," he said. "Let's get you locked away."

"I will be needing extra blankets. At least, if your lockup is no warmer than Dawson's, I will."

"You can rest easy," Graham said. "We won't let you freeze."

6
Scarth Takes Over

Major Aylesworth Bowen Perry, Superintendent Northwest Mounted Police, had a difficult job. Not that there had been any unusual problems during his first hundred-odd days in command, but he knew, more than anyone, how critical most Dawson residents were likely to be of his slightest shortcoming. Sam Steele had left his mark. He had established law in the Yukon, and in Dawson in particular, through an almost unseemly combination of hard-fisted rule and common sense. He had made friends — albeit grudging ones — of most of the very people he held under his thumb. The merchants and saloon-keepers had been on his side; the miners thought him almost a god. Even the whores signed one of the petitions protesting Steele's transfer. He achieved the unusual state of an officer whose men would follow him, literally, anywhere. But Steele had been politically naive, too open and frank for his own good, and now he was gone, had been since the end of September. And Perry had to pick up where Steele had left off.

It was difficult, probably unfair, to be judged by another man's standards but the judgment was inevitable and Perry knew it. He was, at this moment, dealing with his first real test. Major Perry was seated behind a tiny table that passed for his desk in the barracks in Dawson. Across from him sat a man who claimed to be a reporter — one man in four seemed to be a correspondent for something-or-other these days. He was a tenacious fellow with a shock of red hair and a heavy nose that gave him the look — not inappropriately, Perry thought — of a pit bull.

"Well, Major?" the man asked.

"Hmm-m?" said Perry, starting slightly. "I beg your pardon. What did you say?"

"I asked if the police were aware that Fred Clayson is missing and believed murdered." Perry pressed the tips of his fingers together.

"We have, er, received inquiries as to Mr. Clayson's whereabouts," he said.

"Right," said the reporter, drily. "That makes you even with just about everyone in town. Firth got a wire a couple of days ago. You knew about that, I'm sure."

"Er, yes, we had heard rumors to that effect."

"But have you also heard that most people think Fred was murdered?"

"Um ... well ..."

"Come now, Major," the reporter cut in. "Why so reluctant? If murder has not crossed your mind, you are the only person who has not thought of it. Now, do the police suspect murder or not?"

"That is one of the possibilities we are investigating," said Perry. "Not the only one, mind you, merely one of several." The reporter showed no reaction, took no notes.

"So it is possible that Fred was ambushed on the trail?" he asked.

"Possible, yes. Probable, no," Perry replied. "I expect we will find that Mr. Clayson has merely been delayed. But the matter is well in hand."

"What about the other missing men?"

"You are referring to the lineman, Mr. Olsen, I assume. His absence from duty is being investigated."

"Well, he is one of the men I refer to, Major. But, what about the others — Everett and Dumbill, for example — and the five or six others?"

Perry cleared his throat and sat a little straighter. "Investigations are being carried out, sir, with all the resources we have at our disposal."

"Is it true that the police have a suspect under arrest at Tagish?"

"There is a man, er, under arrest."

"Under suspicion of murder?" the reporter persisted.

"That is information I cannot disclose at the moment, sir. I can, however, assure you that investigations are proceeding."

"May I tell my readers that the police have a murder suspect under arrest?"

"You may tell your readers that the matter is under control, that investigations are ... er ... proceeding," Perry said, wishing he could think of another way to state it.

The two men stared at one another across the table. The interview was clearly at an end and the red-headed reporter tucked his notebook, unused, in an inside pocket. He stood.

"I hope we will see an early solution to this problem, Major." Perry stood and bowed slightly. The only reply he could think of was that investigations were proceeding but he was determined not to say that again. So, he said nothing but inclined his head with an air of superiority he did not feel.

As soon as the reporter left, Perry took action: he sent for Inspector William Scarth. There had been, in fact, precious little information about the missing men — a handful of wires from the south, a hundred rumors in Dawson. But, now that the papers were nosing about, something concrete had to be done: act immediately, get some men on the ground, be visible, show decisive action. Inspector Scarth was therefore detached to command the investigation into the missing men, however many there might prove to be. He was given authority to call in as many men as needed, including men of the Yukon Field Force, if necessary. If the stories of ambush were found to be groundless, so be it, but until then there would be a full effort. But Scarth had much to organize, and it was doubtful whether he would be at Selkirk to take charge much before the end of the month. In the meantime, Major Perry knew that the papers would be raising Cain and he would simply have to ride out the storm. And the first sharp breezes were not long in coming.

The Dawson *Daily News* of 8 January had carried a short item entitled "Where is Clayson?" It merely noted that Fred Clayson was overdue and that a wire had been sent by his brother, asking about him. On Tuesday, 9 January the *Daily News* headline read "Were They Murdered?" The story made it clear that the newspaper people knew as much about the missing men as did the police. And, what the writer did not know, he was quite capable of inventing. Clayson, Olsen, and Relfe had been last seen at Minto, the story read, and had not been seen since. The story went on to say that one Tom O'Brien had been arrested at Tagish a few days after Christmas and J. Graves, thought to be O'Brien's partner, had been arrested at Whitehorse a few days later. Not all of this was news to Perry but he had got no word of the second man's arrest. He had a message sent inquiring about this and, in due course, got a reply confirming the arrest of O'Brien's partner.

At 11:25 P.M., the *Daily News* issued an extra in which the question — "Were They Murdered?" — was now an assertion: "Murdered on the Trail. Three Men from Dawson meet with Foul Play". The story repeated information from the first edition but was a good deal more definite about O'Brien's role than the police were prepared to be. The story read:

> The connection of the two ex-convicts with the murder of these three men is formed through a chain of circumstantial evidence that is being strengthened with every day's development. Tom O'Brien and J. Graves both served time in the barracks prison at Dawson. Both are hard cases and O'Brien has the reputation of being a cold-blooded, desperate character who, while in jail, made repeated threats of what he would do when he got out. He broke jail once but was recaptured and given the ball and chain . . .

The story also mentioned Charles Everett and James Dumbill of the Alaska Meat Company who had left Dawson on the sixth of December and had not yet reached the outside. Major Perry read this with some interest because the red-headed reporter had mentioned Everett and Dumbill as being among the missing men. No inquiries about either man had been received by the police.

But it was in the *Daily News* of 10 January that the hand of the red-headed reporter became clear. The paper ran an editorial that reiterated ever more forcefully what was known — and suspected — about the three missing men. Then it concluded. "It is to be hoped that Major Perry will now make a most complete investigation of this terrible state of affairs and devise some plan by which, either by registration at the various posts or some other such scheme, some degree of security to life, limb, and property will be given to the people on the trail."

Criticism of the police was far more blunt in the stores and bars of Dawson. But, whatever Major Perry was, he was no coward. As concern spread in the town he took more frequent tours, on foot, jostling in the saloons, being visible. And he ordered his men to do likewise. None of the policemen had much to say, for the excellent reason that they knew next to nothing about the supposed crime. But, they replied to all questions, however rude, with reassurance. And to all, it was clear that their control — in Dawson anyway — was as firm as it had ever been.

More stories surfaced. George Russell was missing. So was Henry Marymont from Victoria. But the police remained firm: everything was under control, investigations were proceeding satisfactorily. And the storm began to abate. In the *Daily News* of 10 January, alongside the main item about murdered travelers, was a terse note that took the bite out of everything else. A message had been received from Skagway: Everett and Dumbill were safe. The peak had passed. Secrecy was beginning to descend on the investigation and the only new information that the *Daily News* could scratch up was from civilian travelers.

One of these described his trip into Dawson and, in particular, told of the trail between Minto and Hootchikoo. There was an open patch of water, he said, near Minto. It was close enough to the trail for bodies to be slipped into it with ease and it was a good, big hole — fifteen feet wide by fifty yards long — with solid ice right to the edge of the hole. The traveler speculated that the three men were killed near the hole and then disposed of in the deep, swift water.

This same hole held the attention of Scarth and Pennycuick for some time, too. They were interested in the hole, not because the *Daily News* had made so much of it, but because, in the beginning of the investigation, it was obvious that the quickest way to establish the fact of murder was to find the bodies. And the open patch of water was a perfect spot to dispose of corpses. To their great delight, the two policemen found traces of blood near the edge of the hole. It was a tiny bit of blood, to be sure, only the few drops needed to pull crystals of snow into small lumps. But it was definitely blood and it was easy to imagine, what with the heavy clothing the men must have been wearing, very little blood would leak out, no matter what sort of wound was inflicted. So, with the initial flush of excitement, the policemen scoured the trail and river ice and unbroken snow around the big hole. But, after three days, they had exactly the evidence they started with — a few pellets of blood-soaked snow.

When it became clear that this case was not simply a matter of removing a smoking gun from a killer's hand, or of meeting Clayson, Olsen, and Relfe on their way back from staking some remote stream, Inspector Scarth paused to take stock. There was, of course, only the slimmest of chances that the matter would be solved quickly and cleanly, but Old Man King had turned himself in to the police and one could hope for such a thing again. Certainly the Major would be relieved by a quick solution but, evidently, it was not to be.

Scarth and Pennycuick sat off by themselves in a corner of Agnes Fussell's dining room in Minto. It was not as private as one might have wanted but, until other quarters could be arranged for Scarth, it would have to serve.

"This fellow they have in cells at Tagish, what's his name?"

"O'Brien, sir."

"Yes, O'Brien. Do you think he is your cache thief?"

"I will not know positively until I see him, sir," Pennycuick replied. "Some things about the man do not correspond to the man I knew as Miller."

"Such as?"

"The name, obviously. The horses and bobsled. The fact of his being alone."

"But his partner has been arrested."

"Mm-m, yes, sir, so I am told. But I also have heard that he is raising one unholy row about being arrested. He claims he is innocent and has done so from the beginning. Quite unlike O'Brien, I understand."

"Oh? And what does he say?"

"Nothing at all, sir. Not a word. He knows nothing; he has seen nothing." Scarth picked thoughtfully at the largest of the scabs on his lower lip. The hours searching on the ice had given him sunburn and his lips were blistered and cracking. He winced as he pulled the scab off and dabbed at the bleeding spot with his tongue.

"If O'Brien is your man Miller, could he be a murderer?"

"Was he capable of it, do you mean?"

"Yes." Pennycuick thought a moment.

"Miller was a surly and furtive man," he said. "He was a sneak. But I would not have thought him a killer. Unless he were able to kill from ambush, say. I doubt he would have the stomach for it if there were any risk to himself.

"But, with respect, sir, aren't we getting ahead of ourselves? I can tie Miller — or O'Brien — to cache theft but there is nothing connecting him with anything else. Indeed, we really have no evidence that a murder has been committed."

"The newspapers are quite certain," Scarth replied, drily. "And so is Corporal Ryan."

"That is true, sir."

"But you do not believe it? You can be quite frank."

"It is not that I don't believe it, sir. Of course, I will discount the newspaper stories out of hand. And I am inclined to take the Corporal's views seriously. After all, he knew Mr. Olsen well and I did not. If he claims Mr. Olsen was a steady man, I believe him. But there is no *evidence*, sir. That is my point."

"All right. Let us look again at what we have. The three left here on the morning of the twenty-fifth. Right?"

"Yes, sir."

"They did not arrive in Hootchikoo where — am I right — only Olsen was expected."

"Right. They apparently teamed up here Christmas Eve. But Corporal Ryan knew nothing of the other two."

"Fair enough. Now, by coincidence, we also have your cache thief and, presumably, his partner, at a cabin between Minto and Hootchikoo at just the same time."

"No, sir, we do not know that. We are certain nobody was at the cabin after the twenty-eighth or twenty-ninth. But he may have been there two weeks before and was long gone upstream by Christmas Day. We just do not know."

"Well that, obviously, is something we shall have to find out, isn't it?"

"Yes, sir."

"Finally, we have the blood near the open water." Scarth ruefully licked his lip. "Where we have had so little luck."

"But, if I may, sir, I must emphasize that it is the only indication we have of violence being done anywhere along the trail. I believe we must continue to search there."

"I agree. You will do that. But, I must know more about this O'Brien fellow. I take it there was nothing in his personal effects that belonged to the missing men?"

"I do not believe there was, sir."

"Well, I want them checked again. I also want messages sent to every post between Dawson and the outside instructing them to check every roadhouse, camp, cabin — the lot. We must be able to pinpoint a date that O'Brien was here. And when you draft the message for Tagish, have them search O'Brien's property again, as I said. Include all the information you think might help identify our man. Draft the messages as quickly as you can and I will send them over my name."

"Yes, sir. I will have them done within the hour. And will we be on the ice again tomorrow, sir?"

"You will. I am going up to Selkirk for a few days. I have ordered Corporal Ryan to help you. He will be here the day after tomorrow, although, Heaven knows he has enough to do at Hootchikoo. We will not be able to post any more men here, unfortunately."

"I believe we could hire Napoleon Venne for a time, sir. He is a useful man to have."

"Good enough. Get him. But, right now — the wires, if you please."

"Yes, sir."

And so began the long and tedious business of tracing George O'Brien's movements. The police in Dawson knew when he had been released from jail, the police in Tagish knew when he had been arrested and Pennycuick had seen him early in December. There had to be other people who had seen him and those people had to be found. This was no small job because O'Brien had already used one other name — assuming that Miller and O'Brien were the same man. He may have used others. Besides, people came and went by the hundreds; who cared about names, who paid attention? Nonetheless, people were questioned, camps were visited, hotel registers were read.

In Tagish, George Graham searched O'Brien's gear again. He found a dark stain on the dogsled which could, possibly, be blood. But, even if it were, it was hardly incriminating. Tom Dixon began the process of back-tracking at Jennie Murphy's. Did she know O'Brien from before? No. Who had he been traveling with? Nobody. Why was he at her house? To get his dog. How did she happen to have the dog? O'Brien let her use the dog. Why? He thought she looked tired. But she had never seen the man before that? No.

Dixon's investigation did, however, uncover some details about O'Brien's horse going through the ice. He found that O'Brien had stopped at Tagish Charlie's roadhouse the night before his arrest. Frances Chambers, who had charge of Charlie's household, remembered O'Brien arguing with Billy Ensen about feeding the black team. O'Brien claimed that Billy had not fed his horses and, eventually, he fed them himself. In the morning, O'Brien left to cross the river. Chambers said that she warned him the trail might not be safe, that he should take the left-hand trail that led past the police post. But, he went ahead anyway and his horses went through the ice. The Indians pulled the team out, blanketed them, and ran them up and down in front of the roadhouse to warm them. Then O'Brien went on, taking the trail to the police post. Did he seem reluctant to go near the police post? Well, yes. He asked if the police searched travelers. And why else would he have taken the trail across the river?

But, when Dixon questioned Billy Ensen — somewhat sketchily because of Billy's poor English — the story had a different twist. Did the man try to stay away from the police post? No, just a mistake.

He asked which trail and did not understand what I told him. Was he on the wrong trail when he went through the ice? No. I called to him and he was cutting across to the police trail when he went into the river. Did he argue about feeding the horses? Yes. Did he pay you? Yes, he had money. Did he have a lot of money? He had some money and some gold. How do you know he had gold? I saw his poke — it was this big: less than one finger long, two fingers wide. But, did you see gold or just the poke? I saw the poke. Tom Dixon sorted the facts as best he could and wrote his report. It was not obvious to him whether O'Brien had really tried to avoid the police post or not. So, Dixon wrote what he had been told and left the conclusions for others to draw.

In Dawson, nobody remembered O'Brien but the police. And their recollection mostly concerned his escape from jail. Constables Lynn and McBeth had recaptured O'Brien in December of 1898 and returned him to the Dawson woodpile. The records of George Tweedy, Provost Sergeant, showed that O'Brien had finally been released on 16 September 1899. He left with about forty dollars in money and gold dust, a .30-30 Winchester, a robe, a stove, and some smaller articles.

The police in Dawson did get information about Lynn Relfe and Fred Clayson, however. None of the information was spectacular, but they did learn what the men were wearing when they left. And George Noble, a friend of Relfe's, told of a peculiar pear-shaped nugget he had given to Relfe on the day he left. It was unique, Noble said, because it contained a smaller nugget, free to rattle around but inseparable from the larger nugget.

In Dawson, too, the police tracked rumors until they found Auguste Mouquin. Someone had stolen two of his dogs back in November. He had lost a small black dog and a big yellow St. Bernard. Somebody would pay, by God.

Finally, in Dawson, the police found William Levy Powell or, to be more precise, he found them. He had cut the short overland trail between Minto and Hootchikoo to haul his cargo of pork to Dawson. He knew nobody called O'Brien but, when he was cutting the trail, he had encountered a man with a big yellow dog. The man had a rifle, too, and Powell remembered him well.

The reports from Dawson, including Powell's written statement, were passed on to Inspector Scarth who, in turn, gave them to Pennycuick. The information, meager as it was, gave the constable's spirits a lift; it was encouraging to know that someone had some facts about O'Brien. Pennycuick was in need of some good news because that very day, his investigation had taken a large step backward.

As ordered, Pennycuick had been searching near the open water. He had spent long days, half-frozen, scraping in the snow for traces and dragging the river for bodies. He had searched out trails long buried in the snow. He had almost mastered Napoleon Venne's technique for spotting these trails: squatting, hunched, eyes near the surface of the snow, looking for the shadow which the sun cast in the slight depression that marked a trail. But, these hours had yielded not a single piece of evidence. And, to make matters worse, the tiny pellets of blood that had set off the search at this place had, themselves, been proved worthless.

Bayard Burgess had stopped on his mail trip and explained how, at that very spot some weeks before, Ol'Pete had gone foot-sore. It hadn't been much of a cut, really, but you could count on Ol'Pete to act it up for all it was worth, the damned old faker. Burgess had been apologetic. He said he would have told the police sooner but he didn't know what they were looking for. Then, he had shouted at his team and left. Pennycuick had slowly gathered his gear and prepared for the walk back to Selkirk. There was no point hanging around here, he had thought, disgustedly. Dog blood. All that work over a bit of dog blood.

7
The Search Begins

When Pennycuick arrived at the Selkirk Post, Inspector Scarth was there waiting for him. He had had his supper and was sitting, legs stretched out, enjoying a thin cigar that a traveler had given him. He was in fine fettle. Pennycuick straightened and started toward Scarth to report formally but Scarth waved him off.

"Carry on, Constable. Go and warm yourself. And get some supper. Excellent meal tonight." Pennycuick sniffed loudly and began stripping off his frozen mitts and parka.

"Sir?" he queried.

"I say there is a fine meal to be had. Solid, plain food. Just what a man needs." Scarth stretched luxuriously and drew gently on his cigar. Pennycuick looked at him doubtfully.

"Yes, sir," he said. "I very much need a good meal but I will settle for whatever is offered." He rubbed his hands together, gritting his teeth as the blood coursed back through his fingers, bringing waves of pain. Let that be a lesson to you, he thought, forget dry mitts another time and you could lose those fingers. Fool.

"It sounds as if you could use more than a meal," Scarth said. "Have you had no luck?"

"Nothing until this morning, sir. Then I had some luck — of the worst possible sort."

"Oh, so?"

"The blood we found at the hole is dog blood." Scarth straightened in his chair.

"The hell you say!"

"I am afraid so. Burgess — he is one of the mail drivers — stopped at the hole and told me about it. It was his dog. Cut its foot on the rough ice, I suppose. And that was the blood we found."

"And you found nothing else?"

"No, sir. Nothing." Scarth scowled at the ash on his cigar.

"That is a lot of time wasted," he said. "It would not have been

75

too much to ask that the fool mail driver had told us before now, though, would it?"

"I do not think he can be faulted, sir. He was simply minding his business. And we *have* discouraged sightseers and amateurs from cluttering up the area. Burgess had no way of knowing what we were working on."

"Mm-m, yes, I suppose you are right. Dreadful waste all the same." Scarth mused a moment. "I can see how you might be discouraged," he said. "But I have some information you may find cheering."

"Yes, sir?"

"Yes. Pull up a chair," Scarth said, picking up a leather case and extracting a sheaf of papers from it. "There has been a fair amount of investigation of our man O'Brien all along the river. Most of these ..." he indicated the papers "... are from Dawson. And we have word that Tagish is working back along O'Brien's trail. But one of these ... where the blazes is it? ... Ah, yes, here we are. This statement is from William Powell. Do you know him?"

"There was a man of that name hauling meat through here early in the winter."

"That's the man. Well, he came forward in Dawson with a useful bit of news." Scarth frowned at the paper in his hand. "Good grief, look at that handwriting. I must speak to that man — nobody can read this." He leafed through the pages. "Anyway, it doesn't matter; I remember the details. Now, when did you say you met O'Brien on the river?"

"I believe it was 11 December, sir, but I have it in my notes."

"That is what I thought. Well, Powell saw him between the sixteenth and the nineteenth," Scarth said, tapping the sheaf of paper significantly. "And do you know where he saw him?"

"No, sir," said Pennycuick, patiently.

"Right where you were looking." Pennycuick blinked.

"At the hole?" he asked.

"No, not exactly. He saw him at the cabin the Arctic Express people put up."

"Just upstream from the hole?" Scarth closed his eyes and nodded importantly.

"That is good news, sir," said Pennycuick. "At least we have one date for him being in the area. But how did Powell happen upon him? Do they know one another?"

"No. Powell remembered the dog. And when we began inquiries

in Dawson, he heard about who we were looking for and decided he might be of help. Quite an interesting story he told, too."

"Yes, sir?"

"Well, it seems that sometime between 16 December and 19 December — he can't be sure of the date — Powell and his crew were between Minto and Hootchikoo with a load of pork. They ran into some bad ice and one of their teams went through. They spent quite a time trying to make a trail through the rough ice, he said.

"Anyway, while they were working one morning, they saw some activity around the Arctic Express cabin. One man apparently stood guard, watching them, while the other one made several trips out behind the cabin, carrying something. Powell could not see what the man was carrying but he would be gone for ten or fifteen minutes, then he would be back for more."

"The Dalton Trail is back there, sir, behind that cabin," Pennycuick said. "It follows the river. Perhaps he was going to it." Scarth nodded and went on.

"This carried on for most of the morning, Powell said. It was fifty below and yet the man stood watching them the whole time."

"Quite determined," said Pennycuick.

"It appears so. Mr. Powell, however, paid him little attention and did not get a good look at him until the next day.

"The work they did on the river was apparently for naught because they finally decided to go overland and bypass the bad ice altogether."

"And that would be when they cut the Pork Trail," Pennycuick said.

"Exactly. Now, when they were working on the trail, it happens that Powell and his crew were also looking for hay. They had arranged for some at Five Fingers but it had spoiled, apparently, so Powell had wired ahead for more. He was to find it near the Arctic Express cabin. So, while the trail was being finished and his outfit was starting the haul overland, Powell went to find his hay. There was smoke coming from the chimney, he said, so he started across to the cabin. And who should come out to meet him but our friend, O'Brien. He had a rifle which Powell clearly felt he was being threatened with and he asked Powell what he wanted. Powell explained about the hay and O'Brien said there was nothing for him at the cabin and that he should look elsewhere."

"Did O'Brien identify himself?" Pennycuick asked.

"No. But Powell did not stay around because he definitely felt he was not welcome. However, the next day — they were truly desperate for feed, you see — Powell and one of his men went back to the cabin."

"Was there any trouble?"

"None at all. Powell talked with the two men in the cabin — all quite friendly, I understand — and left."

"Did he get their names then?"

"No, but he had a good look around the cabin. There was quite an array of canned food, he said. And he remembered two dogs: a big yellow one and a smaller black."

"That is Miller and Ross," exclaimed Pennycuick. "Or O'Brien and whatever his partner's name is."

"It sounds that way. Incidentally, we have decided to bring O'Brien up from Tagish. I want you to see him when he comes through. If you can identify him as Miller then we will charge him with cache theft for the time being. Your evidence and the rest down the river should do the trick."

"What if he is not the same man, sir?"

"We will deal with that when it arises. In the meantime, I want you to move into the Arctic Express cabin. It is deserted, I understand." Pennycuick nodded.

"Fine. Forget about that open hole and concentrate on the area around the Arctic Express cabin. Search the cabin itself, of course, then make it liveable, set up quarters there. There is a trail behind it, you said? Cover that thoroughly. I want to see what O'Brien and his partner left behind."

"But, sir, with respect, the Arctic Express cabin is an unlikely spot for the murders to have occurred — if there were any."

"And why is that?" asked Scarth, stiffly.

"Because it is across the river from the main trail. And it is a long hike across open ice to intercept travelers, sir."

"That may be. But I remind you that that was the last place O'Brien was actually seen. Correct me if I am wrong, Constable, but he was not *seen* anywhere else from December 19 to the first week in January, was he?"

"No, sir, that is right."

"Certainly. And, as a matter of principle, we will begin working from the evidence we have. It is the only systematic way to do the investigation, So, you will set up camp at the Arctic Express cabin."

"Yes, sir."

"Good," said Scarth, drawing gently at his cigar. "By the way, I understand Corporal Ryan was at the open hole with you?"

"Yes, sir. Both he and Venne were there but they had to leave three days ago. The Corporal had a number of urgent matters to attend to."

"Yes. I spoke to him when he came through here this morning. He had to make a quick trip downriver — something about the cache business again — but he will be back tomorrow. I made it clear to him that this investigation is to be given as much time as he can spare.

"So, the two of you are to set up quarters in the Arctic Express cabin, as I mentioned. Get your gear squared away and be ready to leave when the Corporal gets here. You will be able to arrange for a team, I suppose?"

"I do not know, sir. Is the Selkirk team here?"

"No they aren't, come to think of it. They went downriver before Ryan got here today. I do not know when they are due back."

"Then I will check Vickery, sir. His team is for hire, that is, if he is not otherwise occupied."

"Excellent. Hire him."

"Very good, sir."

"And now, for Heaven's sake get some supper and a night's sleep — you look a wreck."

"Yes, sir."

Corporal Ryan arrived in Selkirk from the north just before noon the next day. Pennycuick had been at work since before daylight, drawing supplies of food and equipment for the trip back upriver. Vickery and his team had been hired; the sled was packed. Ryan had time only to have a quick lunch and get his instructions from Scarth before leaving for the Arctic Express cabin. The trip upriver was fast and hard. Vickery was a skilled and tough driver. His team was fresh and, despite the load that Pennycuick had piled on the sled, they set a killing pace. The policemen, who were anything but fresh, could scarcely keep up.

It was dark by the time they arrived at the Arctic Express cabin. Vickery quickly turned down the offer of lodging with Pennycuick and Ryan, saying Minto was only a few miles back and he would be better off there. He had not questioned aloud the corporal's decision to press on past Minto to a deserted cabin. It did seem a foolish thing to do, but Vickery knew well enough that he had been hired to haul freight, not to offer advice. But his agreement did not include sharing this miserable shack with the policemen. So, he swiftly unloaded the sled and struck back for Minto, leaving the policemen to set up their camp.

Ryan and Pennycuick had doubts about passing Fussell's, too, but the doubts were fleeting. Their instructions had been clear: go to the Arctic Express cabin with all haste and set up camp there. And they had been issued the necessary supplies to do just that. To stay at a roadhouse when there was no call for it could be seen as a frivolous waste of money and, on policemen's wages, they could ill afford to pay for it themselves.

There was no time to stand and think, however. They hauled their supplies into the tiny cabin and, after hunting in the darkness, found a scanty supply of firewood. It might, with luck, last until morning. Ryan lit a fire in the small sheet-iron stove that was the cabin's only fixture. Pennycuick groped among the packs until he found the candles, bread, and tea. He lit a candle and surveyed the new quarters. It was not an encouraging sight. The cabin was small, possibly ten feet square, and dirty. Cracks gaped between the logs, never having been properly stuffed and mudded. The wind pushed through the cracks so freely, it was all but impossible to keep the candle alight.-"Cheery little place, isn't it?" said Ryan, squatting by the stove on which he had placed a tin of snow to melt for tea. "It will be nip and tuck if the stove can melt the snow faster than the draft freezes it."

He looked up sharply as Pennycuick, moving closer to the stove, stumbled and nearly fell.

"Good God, man, watch yourself," Ryan exclaimed. "Are you all right? Here, give me that light before you burn us down. What is the trouble? Are you sick?"

"It is only a chill — only a chill," Pennycuick said. "I suppose I got heated up on the trail."

"Well, you look dreadful. Stay close to the stove there and I will find the bedding." After a brief search he found the blankets and wolf robes which he spread as near the stove as he dared. And Pennycuick crawled into his bed and huddled, chilled to the marrow. When the tea was ready, he drank two mugs of the steaming brew and fell into a cramped sleep. Through the night, the corporal sat near the stove, feeding it wood, listening to the dream-mutterings of his sick partner.

Pennycuick awoke in the icy haze of first light with his joints nearly immobile. His head felt stuffed with raveled rope, his lungs, as if they had been scalded. He moved stiffly and was immediately seized by a fit of coughing. The pain in his chest was terrible. But he forced himself up. The stove was still hot, but Ryan was gone.

Pennycuick went to the door of the cabin. He heard, then, the ring of an axe in the bush and knew that Ryan had gone for wood. He filled the can with snow, set it on the stove and began to walk, painfully, up and back in the cabin, trying to restore the feeling to his feet. Two steps, turn; two steps, turn. As he paced, he thought of the comfort of Fussell's roadhouse, where it was warm, where the cracks in the bunkhouse had been plastered — the bunkhouse they had driven past. Fools. He marveled at the strange and deadly mixture of sensations: face hot and dry, the rest of his body nearly frozen and aching abominably. And now that movement was forcing circulation in his legs, the pain doubled. He thought, in that moment, of desertion, of Mounted Policemen from years past, who had left on the run. And his fevered mind pushed the thought aside. How, precisely, did one escape this frozen hell? There were no walls on Siberian prisons, it was said. And he paced and thought of the man in the Tagish cells. Whoever he was, he was snug and warm and well-fed, the tight-lipped sod. Probably smirking this very minute at the thought of policemen trying to unravel the snarls of his comings and goings. Well, we shall see, you bloody rotter, we shall see. You will cut some wood for your thievery, at any rate. If, perchance, you really did do in Olsen and the others, we will find that out, too.

Pennycuick stopped his pacing to cough, agonizingly. At that moment, Ryan came in with his arms full of firewood.

"Here, what are you doing up?" he demanded, kicking the door shut behind him.

"Getting the feeling back in my legs," Pennycuick replied, hoarsely.

"Well, you look like a corpse. I think we have to get you out of here, so you can be looked after."

"No, I will be fine. Truly. My lungs have always given problems. In a day or two, I will be fit again." Ryan looked doubtful.

"You are certain?" he asked.

"Quite. There is nothing to be done anyway; it must simply run its course." Ryan frowned, pursed his lips, studying Pennycuick's haggard face and fever-bright eyes.

"All right," he said, finally. "But get back to bed. Rest is what you need — that and something to eat."

Ryan fried some pork and bread and as Pennycuick picked

unenthusiastically at the food, brewed a pint of ferocious toddy. The ingredients were tea, sugar, and five ounces of Ryan's precious brandy.

"Take this," Ryan said when he was finished. "It will help knock the fever out of you." Pennycuick took the drink, blew the steam away, and sipped cautiously.

"Go on, now, drink it all," said Ryan. "And be quick about it before the stuff freezes. It's no good if it is cold." Pennycuick quaffed the drink, hacked painfully, and settled back into his blankets. He was asleep in seconds and he slept for the next ten hours.

As the constable slept, Ryan set to work on the cabin. Making as little noise as possible, he plugged most of the larger cracks and banked the walls high with snow. He hunted more dry wood and cut enough for the night. When Pennycuick awoke at six in the evening, Ryan had put some order to the pile of supplies and had a meal ready. He forced his sick partner to eat a little, then gave him another dose of toddy to wash the supper down. During the night, Pennycuick's fever broke and, by morning, he was alert even if he was still unsteady on his feet. His cough, although sharp and barking, did not cause the agony it had the day before and he was able to putter about the cabin while Ryan cut more wood.

The next day, Napoleon Venne arrived and, with his help, the housekeeping chores were quickly taken care of. Then began again the now-familiar routine of searching out depressions in the snow, digging down to the hard layers to estimate when the trail had been packed, and laboriously following the track to see where it had started and where it went. The work was tedious and, it seemed, unending. Venne was almost too good at finding trails. After a week he had indicated a tangled network of paths and tracks, many of them the marks of a lone man, or of a dog team and driver that had passed only once. The number of trails was the more remarkable when one considered that the main traffic was on the other side of the river.

In the maze, however, the men found a fair trail leading back from the cabin. Three or four hundred yards back, it joined the Dalton Trail which was, itself, moderately well traveled. The policemen assumed that these trails were the ones left by O'Brien's partner on his mysterious trips to and from the cabin. But it remained an assumption; there was not the slightest clue as to who had been on the trail or what they had carried. And there was no evidence whatever that Clayson, Olsen , and Relfe had ever been near the place.

Meanwhile, at several points on the river, other policemen were uncovering bits of information concerning the movements of George O'Brien and his partner, as well of the three missing men. Fred Clayson and Lynn Relfe were easy to trace. They were well known in Dawson and their departure was known to the hour; any number of witnesses could be found to attest to times and dates and circumstances. The two men traveled quite openly, of course, and their progress upriver was charted swiftly and accurately through roadhouse registers. At Selkirk, the stories Pennycuick had received from Einar Trana and Charles Dorman were checked and confirmed. As Dorman's story was verified at Minto, it was established — formally this time — that Fussell's was the last roadhouse at which Clayson and Relfe had registered.

George O'Brien and his partner were far more difficult to trace. Registers were no help because nobody knew what names the two men may have used. And physical descriptions were not sufficiently distinctive that roadhouse keepers could recognize in them a couple of men who had passed through early in the winter. But the big yellow dog stuck in the minds of many.

Charles Engquist and Oscar Foglestrom ran the Orange Grove roadhouse, twenty miles below Selkirk. They had seen two men at their lodgings at the end of November. The men had a big yellow dog and a black. Andrew Anderson kept the Meat Cache roadhouse where, in addition to providing board and room for travelers, he kept watch on eight tons of beef for Dumbolton and Gardiner. His roadhouse was fourteen miles above Selkirk and he saw the man with the big yellow dog several times from the fifth to the eleventh of December. He heard the names Miller and Ross but only because he had been present when Pennycuick had questioned one of them; the men had never identified themselves to him. James Fetterley, who had gone with William Powell on his visit to the Arctic Express cabin, remembered both the men and the dogs. But he was no more precise about the date than Powell had been — somewhere between the sixteenth and the nineteenth of December. At Minto, the Fussells both remembered two men with the big yellow dog. The bunkhouse was full on the twelfth of December. The two men had come late and had slept on the floor. Captain Fussell had especially noted the dog because it was a good-natured beast and, as best he could recall, it was the only dog he had ever seen that was called

Bruce. And it was no surprise that Bayard Burgess remembered the dog. He had met two men with the dog on the trail about eight miles below Minto. Burgess was unsure of the date but it was, he thought, about 13 December. At Tagish, miles to the south, no new information had come to light. Constable Dixon had spoken to the Indians, but they had nothing to add to their original stories.

The search back up the trail from Tagish had only begun. As a first step in establishing where George O'Brien had been, however, the police confirmed that the receipt found in his effects was given him at Schock's roadhouse when he bought the team of horses. This was a small point, perhaps, but Graham recalled O'Brien implying that the horses had come from Dawson. Graham searched O'Brien's gear yet again and found nothing.

Then, on 15 February, a powerfully-built man with a great black moustache presented himself at the Tagish post, asking to see George O'Brien. The man called himself a detective and carried a letter from Will Clayson, brother of the missing merchant. The letter stated that the bearer was acting on behalf of Mr. Clayson and asked that he be shown every consideration by the Mounted Police, etc, etc.

The man had talked with O'Brien for half an hour and had then asked to examine the prisoner's effects. There was some reluctance at this but, after a quick discussion, permission was granted, and the man began to paw through O'Brien's possessions. He found the German socks that O'Brien had been wearing when he was arrested. Two quick slashes with a pocket knife and the leather soles of the socks peeled back to reveal two banknotes, each for one hundred dollars. The man smiled a splendid, broad smile and handed the bills to Graham.

"You missed something, looks like," said the man. Graham took the bills and cursed under his breath. Three times through this stuff and never once thought of the soles on the socks.

"Er, thanks," Graham said.

"My pleasure," said the man. "Any time I can help." He turned for the door.

"Are you leaving?" Graham asked.

"Yep. I'm heading downriver."

"Did O'Brien say anything to you in there?" Graham asked. The man shook his head.

"Not a thing," he said, and turned again to leave.

"We may need you as a witness," Graham said. "If we use these bills as evidence we will have to call you. Where will you be?"

"I won't be hard to find. I'll be downriver investigating this case."

"There are policemen down there now, working on it. They are not likely to let a civilian do any snooping around." The man studied Graham a moment, a cheerful twinkle in his eyes.

"Oh, they'll let me work on it all right," he said. "I know you boys are spread mighty thin." He gestured at the money he had found. "And it looks to me like you can use all the help you can get." He smiled and left. Philip Ralph Maguire was on his way to Minto.

On 19 February, Pennycuick and Ryan abandoned their search of the area around the Arctic Express cabin. Three weeks of search had yielded nothing. Pennycuick had gone back to Selkirk. Ryan returned to Hootchikoo, dreading the pile of small matters that would, no doubt, have been set aside for his attention. On Ryan's fourth day back, Maguire, the man with the big black moustache, sauntered in to the post. Ryan was at work on his correspondence.

"My name is Maguire," the man announced. "Philip Ralph Maguire. Will Clayson asked me to look into the business of his brother's disappearance." Maguire took the letter of introduction from his breast pocket and offered it to Ryan. The corporal took the letter, scrutinized it, then looked up at his visitor.

"A detective, you say?" he said. "With Pinkerton's?"

"Nope. I'm my own man. Mind if I sit?" He straddled a chair and, propping his elbows on the chair-back, smiled at Ryan. "I came to give you boys a hand."

"Well, Mr. Maguire, I can only tell you that we have the investigation well in hand. Mr. Clayson was satisfied when he was here looking for his brother and he knows we will keep him posted as things progress."

"But, that's the point, don't you see? It is just about a month since he came through here and he hasn't heard a thing. So I told him I would see what I could do to help."

"Well there has been progress . . ."

"Oh, I know, I know," Maguire said, expansively. "You boys have been digging. And trying to find trace in the snow is like finding flyspecks in the pepper. But, let's be honest; you haven't found very damn much, have you?" Maguire smiled his wide country-boy grin. Ryan found it impossible to take offense.

"No," he said. "We haven't found much."

"Well, there you are," said Maguire. "So another pair of hands would help. It's good to have it settled." Ryan began to say something but Maguire ignored him.

"I've already made a start, by the way. I found some money in O'Brien's socks."

"O'Brien? When did you see him?"

"Oh, about a week ago. I talked with him for a bit in Tagish. Then I found a couple of one hundred dollar notes in his socks. Don't mean a lot, of course, but it might be fair interesting to hear him explain where he got them. He was broke when he left Dawson, I hear."

"Hold on a minute," Ryan said. "Do you mean you found money the police did not find?"

"Yep. Oh, the Staff Sergeant cussed some about it but he shouldn't let it worry him. We all miss things now and then." Maguire stood and rubbed his hands together eagerly. "So, when can we head up the river and have a look around?"

"Well . . ." Ryan said, hesitantly.

"How about tomorrow morning? My team will be raring to go."

The next morning, the two men left Hootchikoo for the Arctic Express cabin. Ryan pointed out the trails they had found. Maguire questioned and nodded and chewed at the ice hanging on his moustache. They spent several days prowling the river, digging in the deep snow, finding nothing. But on the first of March, they scored. Maguire had asked to see the tent-cabin on the Pork Trail. Ryan took him across the river to Powell's trail, then back into the bush where the cabin sat, undisturbed.

Maguire went into the cabin, poking among the loose biscuits and the canned fruit, peering around the bunk. He checked the stove, with its peculiar damper holes. Then, stripping off his mitts, he began probing in the icy ashes of the stove. Suddenly, he grunted and straightened up.

"Well, well,well," he said. "If that ain't the strangest thing."

"What is it?" Ryan asked, craning his neck to see.

In Maguire's hand, fouled with soot and silver ashes, were three moccasin eyelets and a metal buckle.

"Somebody's been burning clothes in this stove," Maguire said, slowly. "Now why would anybody burn clothes in the coldest country on God's earth. A bit odd, wouldn't you say, Paddy?" And Maguire smiled his great, wide smile.

8
Pools of Blood

Finding the eyelets and the buckle in the stove ashes was cause for celebration. Ryan and Maguire whooped and roared and slapped one another on the back. It was an opportune time for dancing a jig, had there been room in the cabin for dancing. The men's jubilation was out of proportion to the value of the items as evidence. There was nothing at all about the eyelets that set them apart from other eyelets and the buckle was a common sort. It was simply that, in sixty-odd days of searching, the buckle and the eyelets — and the peculiar circumstances in which they were found — were the only indicators that the investigation was being made in the right direction. That same day, the men also found a pocket knife, a small, three-bladed effort of unexceptional quality. The owner, whoever he was, had broken a chip from the largest blade and had used a file in a feeble attempt to restore a cutting edge. Finding the knife did not set off a round of foolery as the eyelets and buckle had, but it was far more likely to be identifiable and was, potentially, better evidence.

That evening at the Arctic Express cabin, Ryan and Maguire were able to reflect more soberly on what they had found. Maguire was sprawled on his bed, propped on one elbow. He stabbed the air with the stem of his stubby pipe.

"I say we tightened the screws about half a turn today," he said. "It makes a fellow feel like there might be something out there after all."

"It does," Ryan agreed. "But I am not at all sure what it means."

"Means? Well, I'll tell you what it means: somebody wanted to be rid of a pair of moccasins awfully bad. And what possible reason could he have for that?" Ryan shrugged.

"They could have been worn out," he said.

"Yep, they could have been, in which case you just chuck them away. Did you ever hear of a man burning worn-out moccasins? Did you ever *smell* burning moccasins? A man would be nuts to toss old moccasins in his stove — the stink would drive him out.

"And what about the buckle? Was the belt worn out, too? Come on, Paddy, even if a belt does get a bit tatty, you can always cut it up for smaller straps and laces and what have you. But you don't burn it.

"Nope, I'll give you five to one that stuff belonged to one of your missing travelers." Ryan snorted.

"Safe bet," he said. "We will never prove it one way or the other."

"Maybe. But that's where they came from all the same . . ."

"And that is not all," Ryan cut in. "Even if we could prove whose they were, the eyelets do not prove a crime. We have no bodies, we have nothing that proves a robbery. We have eyelets in a stove. That is peculiar but nothing more. Peculiar things happen every day."

Maguire slowly dug at the contents of his pipe and relit it.

"You're right, Paddy. That is what we need — bodies or some other trace that is good, strong evidence. Now, let's take stock, here." Maguire leaned back on his elbow again, puffing contentedly. "Let's do a little assuming.

"First, we don't need to be concerned about anybody but O'Brien and his partner . . ."

"There is no partner," Ryan said. "The man we picked up in Whitehorse turned out to be the wrong man. He was released two weeks ago or more."

"You don't say. You boys grabbed the wrong man. Tsk, tsk." Maguire silenced Ryan's protest with a wave of his hand. "But, I wouldn't worry about it — mistakes happen all the time.

"No matter. We can confine ourselves to O'Brien, then — he's the only suspect we have. Now, he was seen in this very shack and it's his stove in the tent across the river, right?"

Ryan nodded.

"Good. Now, let's assume he was here for no other purposes than to rob scows and to lift the pokes off travelers. We can be pretty sure that if he killed the three men, it was the last thing he did around here. He wouldn't hang around for a few more days to lift fifty dollars worth of goods from somebody's cache if he'd just killed three men. He'd high-tail it for the outside, wouldn't he?"

"I suppose," Ryan allowed. "Except he didn't seem to be in much of a hurry at Tagish." Maguire scowled, sucked on his pipe, then waved the suggestion away.

"Never mind that for now," he said. "I figure he'd get out of here right smartly. Now we know he used both cabins. The question is:

which one did he use last? If we know that, we know where to look for the bodies. Within a couple of square miles anyway."

"Well," Ryan said. "Powell said O'Brien's partner was hauling something out of this cabin."

"And?"

"And that suggests it was stolen goods being moved out of here for some reason. That is why O'Brien was standing guard."

"So they were moving it back to the Dalton Trail, then upstream a piece so they could hustle it straight across the river to the tent. Very good! They were at the tent last then. They did the robbery from there then beat it up the river. Excellent."

"Yes, that could be," Ryan said, then stopped. "No, wait a bit. We are getting ahead of ourselves here. Powell was cutting the Pork Trail at the time he saw O'Brien here. There was no trail there before and the cabin probably was not there either."

"All the better, Patrick, my lad," Maguire exclaimed. "He had to be at that cabin last because he built it after he moved out of here. Oh, yes, that makes sense.

"Think of this. O'Brien stands guard outside this shack while his partner moves some cache goods back to the Dalton Trail. They are moving, possibly because this cabin is not well hidden, possibly because they think they have worked this area enough. At any event, they are moving. O'Brien is standing here, see, watching Powell and his crew. And what does he see?" Ryan started to speak but Maguire interrupted.

"I'll tell you what he sees. He sees that great slash of rough ice that stopped Powell. The trail there is bad and it will get worse. And there is Powell cutting that handy overland trail that other travelers will use later. It runs right into the bush where nobody can see what is going on. O'Brien sets up on Powell's trail, sits there and waits and ... POW." Maguire smacked his fist into his palm. Ryan started slightly at the outburst. "There, Paddy, what do you think of that?" Maguire sucked wetly on his cold pipe and set about repacking it.

"That is fine," said Ryan, drily. "Except for a couple of points. In the first place, nobody traveled on the Pork Trail after Powell made it. That is a fact: I saw it. Everybody used the river trail just as they do now."

"No matter," said Maguire. "The tent is stashed away back in the bush. It's secret, invisible from the trail. Nobody was going to stumble on him and disturb him."

"That brings me to the other point," Ryan said. "If that cabin was so secret, why didn't he just leave the bodies in it after he robbed them?"

"Well, I . . ."

"My turn to assume," said Ryan. "It was because he killed Olsen and the others some place where he *could* be seen and he was in a mighty rush to get rid of the bodies. So, he stripped them, stuffed them under the ice, packed up the clothes, and drove back to the cabin. There is no risk at all if your sled is loaded with nothing but clothes. At the cabin, he could pick through the pockets and coat linings and the knapsacks at his leisure."

"You boys are determined those bodies are under the ice, aren't you? Even after wasting all that time searching around the big hole."

"You don't agree?"

"Nope. I figure he walked the men up into the bush somewheres. And left them." Ryan shook his head.

"Wrong. That would leave a trail. Stick them under the ice and they are gone. No trail — nothing. And, if you burn all the clothes, the men simply vanish. In fact, that is the only reason I can see for burning the clothes at all." Ryan leaned forward triumphantly. "On top of that," he went on, "If you know you have obliterated all traces of the crime, there is no need for you to run very fast. You can afford to dawdle around in Tagish and lend your dog to Jennie Murphy."

"I don't like it, Patrick," said Maguire.

"You mean the bodies in the river?"

"Not that, because I don't believe they are. But if you are right about his rifling the clothes at the cabin, then the bodies could have been left in the bush just about anywhere along the trail — there is no reason to suppose they are near the cabin, I mean. And don't bother telling me again how they are under the ice. There are no holes handy around here and he damn sure didn't chop one."

"All right, have it your way," said Ryan, resignedly. "But what do we look for now?"

"Bodies," said Maguire firmly. "We must find the bodies. I figure to beat the bush on both sides of the river and the islands until I find them. The tent needs a more thorough going-over but that can wait. And while we are searching the bush, we look out for the stuff they hauled out of this cabin. If they hid it along the Dalton Trail someplace, we will find it. If they hauled it across to the tent, there will be a trail — and a pretty fair one what with a loaded sled and all."

"But only a single track, maybe," said Ryan. Maguire shrugged. "We have found all the other tracks; we will find this one, too, if it's there." Ryan thought of pointing out that Maguire had not yet found a single trail and his use of 'we' was presumptuous. But life was already too complicated, so he held his tongue.

For the next several days, Ryan and Maguire thrashed through the deep snow in the bush looking for trails, looking for bodies, looking for stolen goods. They searched part of the Dalton Trail again, and a small creek that lay near the Arctic Express cabin, and two of the nearby islands. There were no bodies, no caches, and no trails that led to anything useful.

On 12 March Ryan received a packet of messages from Hootchikoo. One of the messages reported a lunatic in a cabin up one of the small creeks. According to the story, two woodcutters had happened upon the cabin and, thinking to go in and warm, knocked at the door. The owner had lunged out of the cabin, swinging an axe and shrieking at the woodcutters to leave him alone. The police would have to see the man.

In the same packet, however, was a wire from Dawson. Inspector Scarth would be at Selkirk on the fourteenth. He expected to meet Ryan there and hear the report of investigations. Ryan pondered which message he ought to respond to. Maguire, ever helpful, pointed out that with a lunatic on the one hand and an officer on the other, Ryan had little to choose. Finally, Ryan decided that Maguire should go to Selkirk, while he would go in search of the madman. He gave Maguire a short written report in which he recommended that Scarth hire Maguire as an investigator and that he be paid for time already spent on the case.

When Maguire arrived at Selkirk, he found Scarth and Pennycuick planning their next trip to the Arctic Express cabin. He gave Ryan's letter to Scarth and immediately showed the two men the eyelets, buckle, and pocket knife he had found.

If Maguire and Pennycuick were wary of one another from first sight, the reasons were not hard to find: each characterized for the other what he least trusted. Maguire had little use for Britishers, especially those in uniform, bowing and scraping and clicking their heels. Yes, sir, no, sir, three bags full, sir. Pennycuick, for his part, saw Maguire as part of the Yankee rabble, different from the mob in Skagway by the fact that he operated, when it suited him, on the right side of the law. But this one was, no doubt, like all American lawmen, separated from the criminal by the haziest of lines.

91

"Where did you say you found this?" asked Scarth, fingering the buckle.

"In the stove in the tent-cabin."

"That would be the same one that you and Corporal Ryan searched, wouldn't it?" Scarth asked, turning to Pennycuick.

"Yes, sir. But we did not conduct a thorough search," Pennycuick said, firmly. "It was the pattern of the stove that interested me at the time."

"Mm-hm," said Scarth. "Well, we have the items now, anyway." Then he turned to Maguire. "The Corporal has high praise for your work, Mr. Maguire. And, as no doubt he told you, he recommends you be hired to work on this case. I will be frank. We need an extra man. You are hired. The pay is not spectacular but it is regular."

"But, sir . . ." Pennycuick sputtered.

"Yes, Constable? You have some objection?" Scarth asked. His tone clearly indicated that he was about to listen to no objection.

"No, sir."

"Good. That is settled then. Let us get down to the matter at hand. What else have you and Corporal Ryan found at the cabin?"

"You see the whole lot right there in front of you," Maguire said, indicating the eyelets, buckle and knife. "That and about a hundred miles of trails. But you know about them, I expect." Scarth nodded.

"I dare say you and the Corporal have discussed this evidence," Scarth said. "Would you be good enough to give us your views?"

Maguire spoke briefly. He told of the possibilities he and Ryan had considered and of their differing views as to where the bodies would be found. When he had finished, Scarth turned to Pennycuick.

"Any comments?" he asked.

"Just one, sir," said Pennycuick. "If there has been murder committed — and I emphasize, sir, that it is still only a suspicion, not an established fact as this fellow has assumed — then the bodies could have been disposed of in a way that seems to have been overlooked."

"And that is?"

"Cremation, sir. Those items, and several others yet undiscovered, may be the remains of burned bodies."

"Nope," said Maguire, promptly. "Bodies are not that easily burned."

"I have *seen* bodies burned," said Pennycuick, precisely. "Bodies are frequently cremated in India and it is done very thoroughly indeed with a simple wood fire."

"And it takes about a half a cord of wood to do it," replied Maguire. "And still there are teeth and bits of bone in the ashes."

"Did you look for such fragments in the stove?"

"Didn't have to. I know there are none there."

"And on what possible basis ..."

"I agree," Scarth cut in. "No bodies were burned. It is much simpler to dispose of them in other ways."

"Yes, sir," said Pennycuick.

"But, I should inform you of some of the latest findings, Mr. Maguire. I was about to tell Constable Pennycuick when you arrived. We have several more reports from upriver where O'Brien was seen at various roadhouses. He had money, it seems, which may be incriminating. He was paying his way at the roadhouses and he bought a team of blacks at Schock's. And our people at Tagish now have two hundred dollars of O'Brien's which they missed — oh, Maguire, I knew the name was familiar. You are the fellow who found the two hundred dollars, I daresay." Maguire nodded and grinned broadly at Pennycuick.

"Of course!" Scarth went on. "They mentioned your name in the wire. Good bit of work, that, although somebody should be jacked up for letting you snoop in the prisoner's effects.

"Anyway, where was I? Oh, yes, O'Brien. Constable Pennycuick saw him, by the way, when the escort brought him through on the way to Dawson. O'Brien and Miller are one and the same man, Mr. Maguire. That helps us a lot.

"But, there is one other bit of information that I have only just received. You will not have heard of this, Mr. Maguire." Scarth turned to Pennycuick. "Do you recall the story out of Dawson about the odd nugget that Noble is supposed to have given Relfe?" he asked.

"Yes, sir. It was described as a double nugget, I believe."

"That is the one. I confess I do not have a clear picture in mind of what the thing looked like. I gather, however, it was most unusual and was remarked upon for that reason. Anyway, in the investigation that has been done from Tagish, one of our men took a statement from a man called Hildebrand. He is the watchman on one of the steamers frozen in somewhere between Bennett and Whitehorse. This Hildebrand claims that early in January a man tried to sell him a double nugget. He wasn't interested and he does not know the man's name. But ...", Scarth paused dramatically, "... he had a yellow St. Bernard."

There was a brief silence, Scarth looking expectantly from one man to the other. Then Maguire struck the table a crashing blow with his fist. "O'Brien has a yellow St. Bernard!" he exclamed.

Scarth smiled and nodded.

"Whooo-ee!" Maguire shouted. "Damn me but that is fine! How about that!" He slapped Pennycuick on the shoulder jubilantly, nearly knocking him out of his chair. "That is the kind of break we needed." Pennycuick recovered his composure and smiled tolerantly.

"That is excellent news, sir," he said.

"Then, gentlemen, we will go back up the river tomorrow. I can only spare two days at the moment but I want to press on around those cabins. Be ready to leave first thing."

When Scarth had left the room, Maguire and Pennycuick said nothing but eyed one another cautiously — like two strange dogs, circling one another, stiff-legged, each waiting for the other to move. At last, Maguire dug out his stubby pipe and began picking at the contents of the bowl with a nail.

"I got the distinct feeling you didn't want to have me around," he said, quietly.

"You are very astute, Yank. We can handle the investigation quite well and I do not approve of squandering money on people of unknown background and uncertain loyalty. If you understand my meaning."

"Oh, I understand," said Maguire, lightly. "But 'the fact is, the Inspector didn't ask you. I don't figure he hired me because of who my folks were or what flag I salute. He hired me because I am a detective. And I'm better than average at what I do."

"We have only your word for that," said Pennycuick.

"That's true," Maguire said, "And that puts you at a disadvantage, whereas I have Paddy's assurance that you are a tolerable handy lad to have on a search — and that is good enough for me.

"But, here's the point. We are going to be stuck in that Arctic Express cabin, you and me, and there is no sense making it more unpleasant than it is already. So, you agree not to call me 'this fellow' or 'Yank', I will promise not to call you 'lobster' and things'll go just dandy."

Scarth, Maguire, and Pennycuick returned to the Arctic Express cabin on 17 March. For the remainder of that day, and the next, they pressed through the bush along the Dalton Trail. It was ground that had been covered twice already but it was covered again at Scarth's insistence. Not having been in the area for some time, he had no feeling for what had been searched and what had not. His questioning about trails that had been proven fruitless began to grate on Maguire and he consoled himself with the thought that Scarth would be leaving for Selkirk the next day.

On the morning of 19 March, Maguire, delighted to be rid of the two policemen for a time, headed upriver from the Arctic Express cabin. If there was a trail across the river to Powell's cutoff, he was determined to find it. He traveled quickly until he had nearly reached Hootchikoo Creek, the extent of the thorough search so far. Then he began again the slow work of trying to pick buried trails out of the snow. By late morning he had reached the creek, followed it away from the river for a quarter of a mile, then returned to the river on the other side of the creek. He found no useful trails. It seemed certain that he had passed the point at which any reasonable man would have crossed the river if he was heading for Powell's trail. Still, Maguire was certain he had not missed the track and he continued upstream.

By early afternoon, he was ready to turn back, sure there was a trail across the river and equally sure he had not passed it. But, if one of his certainties had to yield, it was his belief that O'Brien had crossed the river with a loaded sled. He would revise his theory rather than admit he had missed the track. Then, as Maguire began to puzzle over the suspect's movements for yet another time, there it was: the depression of a sled trail. It cut through the bush, went over the river bank and pointed straight as a string for Powell's cutoff. The trail was far from clear, buried as it was, under two feet of snow, but Maguire knew this was it. He dropped to his knees beside the trail and began to push off the overburden of snow with his hands. He worked down to the packed trail, satisfied himself that it was a sled track and that the sled had been loaded. Then he followed the trail carefully through the scrub to the river. It was an unlikely spot for any man to pick to cross the river. The bank was sharply sloped there and fifty feet high but the trail was easily visible all the way down.

Once on the ice, Maguire realized that the trail was not as straight and clear as it had appeared from the bank. It snaked between the small islands and, on the open ice, had been all but obliterated by drifting snow. With diligence, however, and a sharp eye, it could be followed. By four in the afternoon, Maguire had satisfied himself that the trail led to Powell's cutoff, just below Mackay's cache. He stood at the junction of the main river trail and Powell's cutoff at the spot where, several months before, Prather's dog team had taken the heavy trail overland. It was the spot, too, at which Jennie Prather met George O'Brien as she returned, angry and winded, to the river. Maguire knew nothing of this meeting and, if he had, it would have added little to the satisfaction he felt at having puzzled out a likely sequence of events and, now, seeing the sequence confirmed by evidence.

It was no longer speculation that O'Brien had crossed from the Arctic Express cabin — the track of the loaded sled supported it. And here before him, in the tangle of willow and spruce and cottonwood that covered the bank, Maguire was sure he would find the bodies. With that conviction uppermost in mind, Maguire went back to the Arctic Express cabin for the night.

On 20 March, as soon as there was light enough to see, Maguire was back at the Pork trail. He had his dogs — a husky and a gangling hound — hitched to a lightly loaded sled. It carried only a small grub pack and a shovel; Maguire fully expected to find bodies. He took the right-hand fork on to the Pork Trail and, following the same route he had taken with Ryan, turned right again on the trail which led to the tent-cabin. He moved slowly, confidently, stopping now and then to shovel at a suspicious-looking mound in the snow. He passed the tent-cabin and searched behind in the heavy timber. There was a profusion of dead wood there and much evidence of chopping. This, no doubt, was the place O'Brien cut his firewood and, probably, the logs for the cabin walls as well. But, there were no bodies.

Maguire turned back toward the Pork Trail, taking wider sweeps into the bush. But, still he found nothing. At the junction with the Pork Trail, he turned right again. This part of Powell's trail had been traveled much less heavily but, where the March sun softened the deep snow, the depression of a trail could be seen. He had not traveled more than three hundred yards when he came upon the remains of an old camp from which two trails diverged. The right-hand branch appeared to be more of Powell's work. The left-hand trail, however, seemed to be headed for the river. Maguire took the left branch.

The trail wound through a heavy growth of spruce which

prevented Maguire seeing the river but, after ten minutes' shuffling through the sticky snow, he was sure he was near the bank. Then, to his surprise, the trail branched yet again. The fork was clearly marked by a blazed tree. The left branch of the trail turned sharply left, obviously heading for the bank. The right branch was an even poorer trail than the one he was on but Maguire, curiosity aroused, followed it. He emerged from the patch of heavy timber into clumps of willow through which the faint track twisted and turned. It ran roughly parallel to the river for about a hundred yards then, abruptly, stopped.

Maguire stood for a moment to catch his breath and try to make sense of this odd trail. He was at the edge of the river bank which he guessed was thirty or forty feet high. It was very steep. Around him was thin scrub and a few dead trees but no trace of a trail nor·any sign of bodies. Whoever had come up here had simply gone back the way he had come. What was the point of it? Had he been lost, trying to find the river? There was no way to tell. Maguire turned back. At the blazed tree, he stopped his team and examined the trail that went to his right, toward the river. There were sled tracks — several of them — buried in the snow. And footprints. He turned the team and proceeded down the gentle slope toward the river, following the twists and curves, noting where the trail had been brushed out with an axe, finding two more blazed trees.

Suddenly, as he approached the edge of the river, his dogs stopped, then sprang off the trail, barking, hackles raised. The hound tried to go right but the husky had gone left and was the stronger of the two. The husky, yanking at his harness, dragged the hound back and both dogs and the sled ended in the deep snow to the left of the trail in a hopeless snarl of traces.

"Whoa, there!" Maguire roared. "Confounded mutts." He aimed a kick at the husky, still lunging in the tangled harness. "Quit! What ails you fool dogs anyway? Here, damn you! Come here!" He caught hold of the husky, disentangled him from the harness and chained him to a tree back up the trail.

As he unhitched the hound, Maguire's mind was racing. Bodies — the dogs had smelled the bodies. Had to be. They never behaved like that ordinarily. Must have run them right over the dead men. He tethered the hound, heaved the sled out of the way and began to shovel. There was no mound in the snow so the bodies had to be buried deep. He cleared an area about eight feet square, digging, as usual, down to the packed snow of the trail. No bodies. He moved two feet farther down the trail and dug again, lifting off the overlying snow and setting it carefully aside.

Even with the certainty in mind that he would eventually find the dead men, Maguire's heart leaped when he finally struck the packed snow. It was not a body but it was almost as good. For there, two feet down, was a patch of frozen blood. Not droplets or smudges like those the police had found at the open hole but a pool fully twelve inches across, soaked deeply into the snow, frozen in strings before it could clot fully. This was it; no cut foot had made this pool. This blood had come from a sizable hole in a man's body.

Elated and strengthened, Maguire went on shoveling and, by late afternoon, he had found a second puddle of blood, this one barely twenty feet from the river bank and not more than sixty feet off the main river trail. In the failing light, Maguire carefully covered the blood patches with snow as a precaution against some fool finding them and spoiling his evidence. He hitched his team and led them around the overturned snow, onto the main trail. He looked back at the bank, now deep in shadow, and at the trail over which he had just traveled. Had it not been for the heaps of shoveled snow, the trail would have been invisible to all but the most careful eye. It was, Maguire thought, a fair place for an ambush. He turned and set off for the Arctic Express cabin, feeling very smug indeed.

On 21 March, Maguire again prowled the trails near the tent-cabin. Chapman, one of the men of the Yukon Field Force, had been sent to help him. However, because the man had little knowledge of the area and because Maguire was loath to spend time explaining, Chapman was simply pointed at the bush and told to look for bodies. Maguire himself took the Pork Trail again, this time following it past the branch at the old camp and on to the junction with the river two miles down. This part of the trail was scarcely traveled but it was just possible that, while the men were killed where he had found the blood pools, their bodies were hauled back in the bush for disposal. He worked both sides of the Pork Trail to the end, then came back by the main trail past the high cutbank where he had found the dead end, to the spot where he had found the blood. The entire search — a whole day — produced nothing.

Maguire hallooed for Chapman and, while he was waiting for the man to appear, carefully uncovered the patches of blood and sampled them. He put the pieces of blood-soaked snow in clean jam pots and, with a much-disgruntled Chapman in tow, left for camp.

Riverbank where the bodies were thrown into the river (Public Archives Canada RG 18 vol. 254 File 318 Pt 4)

View of the Yukon River looking upstream from where the bodies were thrown in (Public Archives Canada RG 18 vol 254 File 318 Pt 4)

Pennycuick on the blazed trail showing the route to the river (Public Archives Canada RG 18 vol 254 File 318 Pt 4)

Frame of O'Brien's tent, originally covered with canvas (Public Archives Canada RG 18 vol 254 file 318 Pt 4)

Hootchikoo Detachment (Public Archives Canada RG 18 vol 254 File 318 Pt 4)

George O'Brien as photographed by Scotland Yard (Public Archives Canada RG 18 vol 254 File 318 Pt 4)

Fred Clayson (Public Archives Canada RG 18 vol 254 File 318 Pt4)

George O'Brien after arrest (Public Archives Canada RG 18 vol 254 File 318 Pt 4)

9

The Nicked Axe

In the late afternoon of 21 March, Constable Pennycuick arrived at the Arctic Express cabin where Maguire and Chapman, back from the trails, were splitting a supply of wood. The policeman stood, unnoticed, by a corner of the cabin for a few seconds, listening to the whish and chunk of the axes. Then he spoke.

"Bravo, gentlemen," he said, "That is making the chips fly." Maguire whirled, startled, then relaxed.

"Oh," he said, short of breath, "It's you. Do you have to sneak?"

"Merely keeping an eye on how our money is being spent. And, I must say, Mr. Maguire, you were most diligent." Pennycuick turned to Chapman. "And how are you, Mr. Chapman?"

"Middling," Chapman answered. He blew his nose savagely between his thumb and forefinger.

"Were you in the bush today?" Pennycuick asked Maguire.

"Yep, the whole day. And yesterday, too."

"Did you find the bodies, perchance?" Maguire shook his head.

"I thought you wouldn't," said Pennycuick, drily. "But rest easy. We will get at the job tomorrow and we will make some progress then." He turned away and disappeared around the corner of the cabin. Maguire and Chapman heard a whistle and in a few seconds Pennycuick reappeared leading a big, yellow dog.

"Where'd you get the pup?" Maguire asked, amused. Then he recognized the animal. "Why, that's O'Brien's dog," he exclaimed. "What are you doing with him?"

"Just an idea I have," Pennycuick replied. "You will see tomorrow." He rumpled the dog's fur. "We will put you to work, too, won't we old fellow?"

Maguire had gone to his sled, retrieved one of the jars and removed the lid. He held the jar in his cupped hand so the contents could not be seen.

"Well," he said, "Speaking of what we will do tomorrow, I have a little something here we ought to find out about. Take a whiff and tell me what it is." Pennycuick looked puzzled then sniffed boldly at the small opening between Maguire's hands. He jerked his head away, trying not to grimace.

"It is dead, sir, whatever it is," he said stiffly. "Now, what sort of small joke are you playing?" Maguire chuckled.

"It's no joke," he said. "Look here." He took his hand away to show the frozen clot. Pennycuick's eyes widened.

"Blood," he exclaimed. "You have found blood. Why, that is splendid. Where was it? What were the circumstances?" But Maguire, grinning broadly, shook his head.

"Nope. Not another word," he said. "If I can wait to see your idea about the dog, you can wait to see where I found the blood." And at that he went into the cabin, leaving Pennycuick staring after him. Chapman, hiding a smirk, studied the toe of his boot intently.

On 22 March, Maguire, true to his word, took Pennycuick to the spot where he had found the blood. But he deliberately took the long way around as a test of the policeman's patience. He led the way to the downstream end of the Pork Trail then started along it. He moved at a leisurely pace, giving a formal, and unnecessarily detailed, report of his searches of the previous two days. He pointed out a number of features of the trail, most of them meaningless, and all of them well known to Pennycuick. Throughout all of this, Maguire never let so much as a twitch of a smile touch his lips.

Pennycuick soon realized what Maguire was about but he was determined not to give the satisfaction of showing his impatience. But, neither did he let Maguire's game annoy him overmuch. For, knowing that the blood had been found somewhere near the tent-cabin, he saw the bush and the trail and the lay of the land as if for the first time. And, as he followed Maguire, there was little that escaped his notice.

"Now, just here," Maguire was saying, "You will notice the trail branches. The right-hand branch leads to the cabin, as you know. I searched the bush around the cabin for, I believe, three hours and forty minutes, all told. I found evidence of cutting in the dead wood behind the cabin. And that was all. Then I carried on down the Pork Trail." At the old campsite, they stopped.

"This camp was not searched," Maguire said. "But, at his point, you can see that the Pork Trail continues on while here to the left we have another branch.

"I searched the Pork Trail to its end — its upstream end, I mean — and found nothing. Again we take the left branch. Notice that there has been a fair amount of brush cut to make this trail." Pennycuick nodded calmly and they carried on.

"And at this blazed tree," Maguire said, "the trail branches yet again."

"Did you cut the blaze?" Pennycuick asked, speaking for the first time in half an hour.

"No. Somebody else cut it," Maguire answered. Then, his delight with himself began to well up and he could contain his excitement no longer. "And not only that, look here," he said, heading down the trail toward the river. "Here's another blaze. And another." Maguire was almost running when he came to the spot where his dogs had shied. He dropped to his hands and knees, carefully scraped away the snow he had shovelled over the blood then sat back on his heels. He looked up at Pennycuick.

"There it is," he said, excitedly. "What do you think?" Pennycuick whistled softly, peered closely at the ropy mass.

"That is excellent," he said. "Very good work indeed."

"The other one is over there," Maguire said.

"The other one?"

"Yep. I found two pools."

"You didn't tell me that," Pennycuick said. Then he smiled. "But then you did not tell me much," he said. "Shall we have a look?"

They uncovered the other pool of blood and examined it. In the course of this, Maguire described the last leg of the trail, the part that ended abruptly at the cutbank. Pennycuick insisted upon seeing that, too.

When they arrived at the end of the trail, Maguire turned to Pennycuick.

"This is where it stops," he said. "I grubbed all around there and the trail does not go on. Whoever made it turned back. Maybe he was just lost." Pennycuick frowned.

"I don't think so," he said. "I am willing to wager the bodies went over the cutbank right here."

"Nonsense," snorted Maguire. "Shoot your man twenty feet from the river, on the flat, then haul the body up here over that miserable trail, just to roll him down the bank to the ice again? That's crazy."

"Not at all. This bank is washed away because it protrudes far enough into the river to be battered by the current. The same current may have left open water. Did you look?

"Well, no. You can't see from here and the river trail swings away from the bank, so you can't see from there."

"We will look. And I think we will find open water or, at least, very thin ice. But, first, I want to go over the edge to see what is to be found."

He gingerly slid down the sharp slope, heels digging for purchase in the snow and gravel, until his head was at the level of Maguire's feet. Then, clinging to the roots of undercut trees, he studied the surface of the bank, moving slowly, sending trickles of loose debris rattling down to the ice.

"Be careful you don't slip there," Maguire warned. "There's not much to hold on to."

"You are so right," Pennycuick replied. "Hi. What have we here?" Maguire peered over the edge, saw Pennycuick pull off a mitt with his teeth and pluck something from one of the roots. The policeman shifted his feet for a better hold and squinted at the object, turning it this way and that. Finally, he handed it to Maguire.

"What do you think it is," he asked.

"Looks like a couple of threads out of a sweater," Maguire said, after a moment. "It isn't hair. No, from the way it's wrinkled, I'd say it is out of a sweater." Pennycuick scrambled back on solid ground.

"Maybe the bodies did go over here," Maguire said, handing back the threads. As he did so, a puff of wind snatched them.

"Oh, Lord. I have dropped them," Pennycuick cried, vainly trying to follow the threads as a naturalist might fix his eye on a rare butterfly. He lunged, clutching with his bare hand, nearly pitching over the edge in his attempt to trap his precious evidence. But the tiny bit of fluff was gone.

"Sorry," Maguire mumbled, "I should have hung on to them."

"Not at all. My fault entirely," Pennycuick said. "But it is no great loss; we both saw them and we can describe what we found."

They lost little time mourning the loss of the threads; there were other, more important, things to consider. As the men made their way back up the trail past the blazed tree, Pennycuick pointed to stumps and cut branches.

"Look at them," he said. "Of all the cutting that has been done, none of it has been done with a keen axe. Did you notice that? See, there is another stump. It looks to have been bruised off rather than cut." Maguire, as a matter of fact, had not noticed this before. But, now, he checked every place that the trail had been cut, and the blaze on the tree as well. It was a fact that the brushing out had been done with a dull axe.

"And you can see the contrast when we look at stumps on the Pork Trail and along the telegraph line," Pennycuick said. "There the cutting has been done cleanly. But, before we check that, I want to see something at the old camp. Since you did not mention it to me, I assume you did not see it."

"What's that?" Maguire asked.

"Come along."

When they got to the old camp, Pennycuick indicated the bush with a sweep of his arm.

"Tell me what you see," he said. They stood in a small clearing where the Pork Trail branched. Maguire looked slowly around. There were the poles that had once supported a lean-to tent and little else to be seen.

"Well, I don't know what you mean," he said "I told you I didn't search the old camp. It's obviously been there for years. It has nothing to do with this case."

"I agree," Pennycuick said. "But what I have in mind has nothing to do with the old camp."

"And I can see the stumps that Powell left."

"That is not what I meant either. Keep looking." Maguire turned studying the snow and trees. Then he stopped. He realized he could see the river. He could see downstream to the junction of Powell's cutoff with the river trail, and well beyond.

"Well, I'll be . . .," he said. "A man can spy out the whole landscape from here. He could stand on this spot and watch anybody coming from Minto. He'd see them as they came around that island. And, what's that — a mile? Maybe more?"

"More than a mile, I should say," Pennycuick answered. "But, go on."

"Blast! It's as plain as can be," Maguire exclaimed. "Why didn't I see it before? Standing here, a man could see whether travelers took Powell's trail or stuck to the main trail. If they came up Powell's way, they'd walk right by, just like I told Paddy. If they stayed on the river, he'd have plenty of time to hustle down to the blazed tree and sit waiting for them."

"Good. I was sure you would notice it, too," Pennycuick said. "But, I especially want to look at some of those trees." He pointed along the line of clear view. "I expect that at least some of the downed timber was cut because it obstructed the view."

The men left the trail and waded through the deep sticky snow to the fallen trees. They examined five. All had been felled, untidily, with a blunt axe.

In the afternoon, Maguire and Pennycuick returned to the trails, this time in the company of Inspector Scarth and Constable Buxton. Scarth had come back to check on progress and, as usual, had insisted upon seeing for himself everything that Maguire had found.

They made their way up the Pork Trail with Maguire leading and Pennycuick bringing up the rear with O'Brien's dog. At the old camp, Maguire was showing the view of the river when Pennycuick released the dog.

"Go home!" he said. "Go home!" The dog looked bewildered.

"Go on, then, go home!" The other three men looked at Pennycuick strangely, but, when the dog finally turned and trotted back down the trail, the point was suddenly clear.

"That's it, go on!" Maguire urged.

"Hah! Get out of it!" shouted Scarth. The big yellow dog stopped, confused, then ran back to Pennycuick.

"If you don't mind, gentlemen, I had better handle him," Pennycuick said, patiently. "He is accustomed to me and I think you frighten him." He stroked the dog to calm him, then sent him home again. This time, with no conflicting voices to contend with, the dog ran back along the Pork Trail and, without hesitation, turned onto the trail that led to the tent-cabin.

When the men got to the cabin, the dog was already there, lying contentedy under a tree nearby. There was a wire wrapped around the trunk to which a dog could easily be tethered.

"'That is just what I hoped for," said Pennycuick, happily. He turned to Scarth. "You see sir, we had so little evidence linking O'Brien with the cabin — just the stove, really. I thought it possible that the dog had lived long enough here to remember the place as home."

"I would say he is at home, all right," said Scarth. "Yes, he clearly has been here before." Scarth walked back to the tent-cabin, inspecting the log walls closely. He pulled loose a corner of the canvas cover and grunted to himself.

"So, this is O'Brien's hideaway," he said at last. "The cuts on the logs look fairly fresh. When do you reckon he built it?"

"We are not certain, sir," Pennycuick replied. "But, at a guess, about the middle of December, just after Powell cut the trail."

"And you are quite certain the canvas came from Mackay's cache?"

"Not absolutely, sir. We know there is canvas in the cache but we have not tried to match this bit with it. That is one item on a long list of things we have yet to do."

"Mm, yes. Well, see to it as soon as you can." Scarth went inside the cabin. At that moment, Maguire, who had been out of sight on the other side of the cabin, returned. He had his hands full.

"Look what I found," he said, brandishing a double-bit axe. "It was half-buried there in the snow." Pennycuick took the axe and inspected the edges.

"It is certainly blunt enough to be the one used on the trails. Look at the nicks in the blade, will you." Then he went to a corner of the cabin where the cut faces of the wall logs were exposed. He shifted the axe head around until it coincided with one cut in the wood. "And it is not surprising to find that these nicks in the blade have left their marks in the wood," he said. "Not surprising, but encouraging, nonetheless."

"So, the cabin logs were cut with this axe?" Maguire said.

"Of course," Pennycuick said, carelessly. "You would have been astounded if they had not been, would you not?"

"Yeah, I suppose. But we may be able to get the axe identified." Pennycuick shrugged.

"It is possible," he replied, "But I think it unlikely. The axe may be listed among O'Brien's effects in the Provost's record in Dawson but the entry will say 'one axe, double-bit'. And who remembers axes? But, we will check it anyway."

"And I kicked this out of the snow, too," Maguire said, handing over a bottle. Pennycuick rubbed a bit of crusted snow from the label.

"Hmph," he said, reading the label. "Hudson's Bay Company West India Lime Juice." He pulled the cork and sniffed. "Whiskey," he said. "The bottle had whiskey in it. Now, this could be useful. It was undoubtedly sold at one of the roadhouses. It could be a lead."

Scarth came out of the cabin, ducking to avoid the low doorframe.

"You are quite sure about that stove are you?" he asked.

"Yes, sir," Pennycuick replied. "I saw that stove in the Hell's Gate camp."

"Or one like it," Scarth corrected him. "When I get back to Dawson, I will have inquiries made of the tinsmiths. We will want to know if the pattern is unique." He looked inquiringly at the bottle Pennycuick held. "What do you have there?" he asked.

"Whiskey bottle, sir. Empty. And an axe. They were in the snow over there." Scarth took the bottle and looked closely at the label.

"I do not see any marks on this bottle indicating who found it, or where, or when. The next time I see this bottle, it *will* be so marked or I will be most annoyed. Everything that is found here will be properly marked and recorded in your notes. There will be a trial in this matter — if all goes well. And I do not want either of you stumbling about, unable to identify an exhibit because you did not mark it or record it. I would call that negligence and, by God, I will deal harshly with it. Am I clear?"

"Yessir," said Pennycuick.

"Right," said Maguire.

"Excellent. Systematically. That is how I want the investigation done, gentlemen. Systematically."

"Yessir," said Pennycuick. Maguire said nothing, totaly absorbed as he was in picking at a loose thread on the cuff of his coat.

On 23 March, Maguire and Pennycuick were gathering the equipment they needed to continue searching the trails. Scarth and Buxton had left half an hour before, much to Maguire's delight.

"It's not that I dislike him, exactly," Maguire said, "And I daresay he's a good policeman. But it is a pain in the backside when he just drops in and you have to go over all the same ground again and explain what trail goes where and what you think it means. And he sticks that damn glass in his eye and squints at you like it wouldn't matter what you had found, it would only be half good enough."

"Hm, yes," Pennycuick said, cautiously. "But remember he is directing the search along the entire river."

"Oh, I know that. But he is just so ... oh, I don't know ... overbearing, I guess. Like the business about my not marking the whiskey bottle. I had only just dug it out of the snow, for Pete's sake. And the little lecture about being able to identify exhibits. We both know about all that. What does he think we are, children?"

"No, he doesn't," Pennycuick said, soothingly. "He had a point to make and, I might say, he is quite right about the exhibits. He chose to make the point in a dramatic way, shall we say. But the point was made and neither of us will forget it."

"Hmph," said Maguire.

"But if you still think he treated us like children, I remind you he has left the search completely in our hands." Maguire brightened somewhat at that.

"True enough," he said. "So, how do we do it?"

"Systematically," said Pennycuick, grinning slyly.

"Oh, of course," said Maguire, drawing himself up and squinting in a fair imitation of Scarth. "That is how I want the investigation done, gentlemen. Systematically."

"Mind you, we can poke fun all we like," Pennycuick said. "But yesterday, Inspector Scarth was only overbearing; you would not like to meet him when he was annoyed."

"I believe that," said Maguire. "Not that I care a hoot for what he might do to me — beyond stopping my pay, that is. But, you are right. Systematically, it is. Where do we start?

"I have been thinking about that," Pennycuick replied. "Here is what I propose. First, we clear the trail where you found the blood. Cut a strip four feet wide, down to the level of the old snow, and stack the shovelled snow carefully to one side."

"You mean shovel the whole trail?" Maguire asked, incredulous.

"Yes. From the river to the blazed tree."

"But that must be a hundred yards."

"It is more than a hundred yards — closer to one hundred and twenty, I should say. But I believe it must be done."

Maguire thought a moment, then nodded reluctantly.

"Agreed," he said.

"Good. Now, the trails — all of them — must be measured. I believe I can locate a surveyor's chain without much trouble. All of the distances will be charted and all items we find will be plotted on the chart. Everything, whether it seems useful or not, will be marked and recorded in our notes when we find it. We will package whatever we find in an appropriate manner and send it to Inspector Scarth at the first opportunity.

"I suggest that we leave no exhibit material on the site but, rather, use small, labeled sticks to mark the location of each item. That way, if we have busybodies prowling about, our sticks could get mixed but the evidence will be secure.

"The ice at the foot of the cutbank is to be cleared, opened, and the river is to be searched for the bodies. Soldiers from Selkirk will be sent down and we can put them to work cutting ice.

"Is there anything I have overlooked?"

Maguire shook his head. "Not that I can think of," he said. "I'm sure it won't satisfy ol' smokin' Billy but he shouldn't have cause to be annoyed." Maguire snapped his fingers. "Oh, yeah," he said, "I knew there was something; fix a spot for a latrine." Pennycuick raised his eyebrows in question.

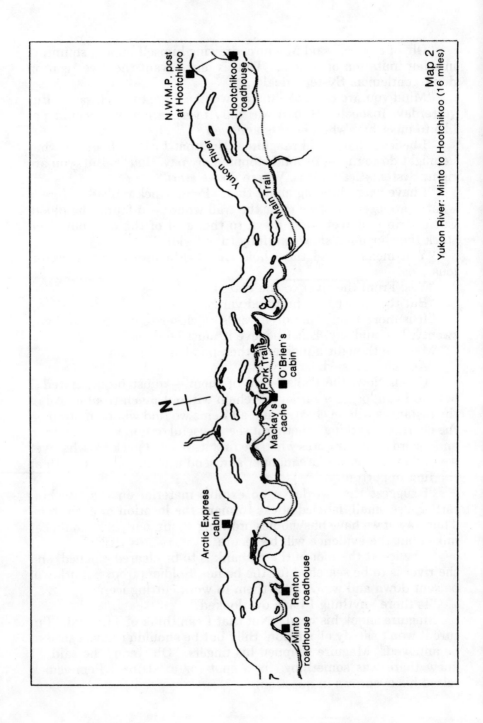

N.W.M.P. post
at Hootchikoo

Hootchikoo
roadhouse

Yukon River

Main Trail

Pork Trail

O'Brien's
cabin

Mackay's
cache

N

Arctic Express
cabin

Renton
roadhouse

Minto
roadhouse

Map 2

Yukon River: Minto to Hootchikoo (16 miles)

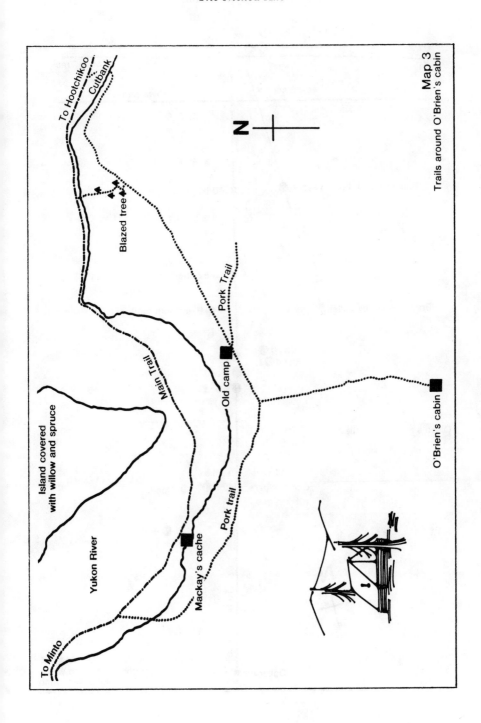

Map 3

Trails around O'Brien's cabin

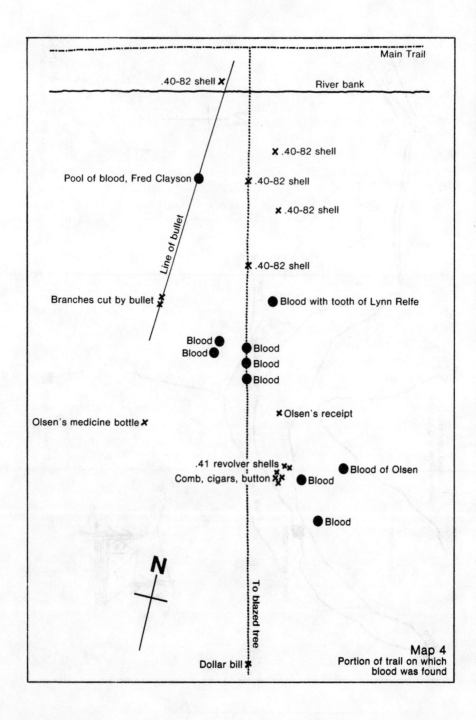

Main Trail

.40-82 shell ✗

River bank

✗ .40-82 shell

Pool of blood, Fred Clayson ●   ✗ .40-82 shell

✗ .40-82 shell

Line of bullet

✗ .40-82 shell

Branches cut by bullet ✗✗   ● Blood with tooth of Lynn Relfe

Blood ●
Blood ●   ● Blood
          ● Blood
          ● Blood

✗ Olsen's receipt

Olsen's medicine bottle ✗

.41 revolver shells ✗✗
Comb, cigars, button ✗✗✗   ● Blood of Olsen
                    ● Blood

                    ● Blood

N

To blazed tree

Dollar bill ✗

Map 4
Portion of trail on which
blood was found

"No. I am serious about that," Maguire said. "We are going to be up there a long time and we don't know where we might want to dig. But I do not want to find any revolting surprises in the snow."

"I agree," Pennycuick said.

So began the search — the systematic search — of the trail on which Maguire's dogs had found the pools of blood. And the object of the search was simple: to find whatever physical evidence there was to help reconstruct the events of Christmas morning, 1899.

The police had long since abandoned hope of a clear-cut solution to the case — such as a confession, for example. George O'Brien had said little on his arrest and had said even less since. He appeared perfectly content to return to Dawson, face the charge of theft, serve his time on the woodpile, and be gone. The possibility was not remote that he would be gone before any other charge could be brought against him.

It was certain that Clayson, Olsen and Relfe had disappeared — Relfe's family had joined with the Claysons in offering a reward for information as to the fate of the men. The police knew where the men were last seen and when, almost to the hour. But there were no bodies and the disappearance, in and of itself, was no more than suspicious, despite the trumpeting of the Dawson press.

It was certain that O'Brien had been in the area of the Pork Trail shortly before Christmas but that could be easily explained by the location of Mackay's cache. And, once O'Brien had been tried for cache theft, he would need no further explanation of his movements.

It was a fact that O'Brien had more money when he was arrested in Tagish than he had when he left Dawson. But that was only slightly suspicious — men came by sizable sums in a variety of ways, not least of which was selling stolen cache goods to roadhouse proprietors.

It was certain that the pools that Maguire found were, indeed blood. And, while to the police, that was solid evidence of foul play, there was no illusion about how long the fact of pools of blood would remain significant, given the attention of a reasonably competent lawyer.

"You claim these patches were blood. Is that correct, Constable?"

"Yes, sir."

"But you do not know the origin of this blood."

"I suspect it to be human."

"You suspect? Do you know, of your own knowledge, that the blood was human?"

"No, sir."

"Of course you don't. But is it not a fact, Constable, that animals are hunted for food in this territory?"

"Yes, sir."

"Hunted on the very ground on which you found this blood?"

"I suppose so."

"And what does a hunter do, Constable, having shot an animal?"

"He dresses it."

"Certainly, but even before that, what does he do?"

"He sticks it."

"Of course he does. He cuts the animal's throat. And the animal bleeds, doesn't it?"

"Usually."

"Yes and the blood would run into the snow, making a pool, wouldn't it?"

"Yes."

There was, of course, the curious nugget mentioned by George Noble and James Hildebrand. That could link O'Brien to Relfe but the nugget had not been found. That, in itself, was not insurmountable; the nugget need not be physically present to be useful evidence. But everything then depended upon Hildebrand's recollection of the thing, having seen it only once for a few seconds. Nobody knew what sort of witness Hildebrand would be.

So, Maguire and Pennycuick began a detailed search of the snow in the knowledge that a case could be made only by illuminating the events that had taken place on the trail. If the events could be reconstructed at all, it would have to be from physical evidence left behind, the bits and pieces, the tiny things that accompany every crime. They needed to find the insignificant facts which, when taken one at a time, mean nothing but, when presented together, interconnected, admit of one explanation and one only.

10
The Broken Tooth

That day, 23 March, Maguire and Pennycuick opened the trail from the river to the blazed tree. They scooped the overlying snow down to within a few inches of the level on which the blood had been found. Including the extra work needed to clear the area around the two blood patches, they moved almost two hundred cubic yards of snow. Then, on hands and knees, they picked and scratched at the remaining snow with small sticks, moving it as carefully as an archaeologist might, working down to the trail that had been made three months before.

As a matter of convenience more than anything, Pennycuick chose as his reference the point at which the trail met the river ice. By this reckoning, the first pool of blood was located eighteen feet from the river and six feet six inches to the right of the center line of the trail. The second pool of blood was forty feet six inches from the river and one foot six inches to the left. As they worked up the trail, however, they found more blood spots, so many more, in fact, as to be almost an embarrassment.

There were three in the center of the trail: at forty-nine feet, six inches, at fifty feet six inches, and at fifty-two feet six inches. The latter pool was the largest. However, as the two men cleared the area around the latest finds, they encountered two more spots. These were a foot apart, forty-nine feet six inches up the trail and three feet to the right. Nor was this all. Ten feet farther down the trail and six feet to the left was a group of three blood spots, within a few feet of one another. These lay among clumps of willow that intruded upon the trail from the left.

Maguire muttered about it being either feast or famine on that blasted trail then stopped, ashamed of the ghoulishness of what he had said. Still, the cluster of eight blood spots presented a puzzle. It was easy enough to imagine two of the men being killed, one each at the blood pools nearest the river. But that left only one man to account for this last quantity of blood, and that spread all over creation.

It could mean that the body was dripping blood when it was being moved, thus staining the snow in several places. But it could also mean that the third man did not simply drop and die but fell and rose and fell again in an attempt to evade his attacker. Maguire even went so far as to speculate that the quantity of blood, its distribution, and the numerous footprints that were uncovered around the patches suggested that the man had been killed with a knife or an axe. The third man, according to this theory, had been pursued and hacked at until finally being run to ground in the willows.

The axe theory was discussed until the middle of the afternoon when Pennycuick, searching at the blood nearest the bank, found an empty cartridge. It lay in the center of the trail. When Pennycuick shouted, Maguire ran back to see what he had found.

"What caliber is it?" he asked, excitedly.

"It is a .40-82 Winchester," Pennycuick replied. "It will fit the rifle Corporal Ryan found in the tent."

"Blast!" said Maguire.

"What is wrong with that?"

"I'd be a lot happier if it was a .30-30. That's what O'Brien carried."

"Oh, come now. You can't have everything. We have placed him in the tent where the rifle was. And here is an empty."

"Right. Of course," Maguire said. "So it means somebody was shooting. I suppose that is a good start."

"But, wait a bit. It is more than a start. Look at it. Olsen and the others have been herded off the main trail — whether at gunpoint or through some subterfuge, I cannot say. But, they have clearly started up the trail toward the blazed tree. Suddenly, from behind, they are cut down by a fusilade of rifle fire."

"Whoa," said Maguire. "One empty cartridge does not mean a fusilade."

"Of course not," Pennycuick went on, enthusiastically. "But, there are other cartridge cases to be found, I am sure. And, obviously, the man who thrashed about up the trail there was not killed with one shot. No, I am convinced there was a good deal of firing here for a few minutes."

"Suppose there was. What of it?" Pennycuick grinned gleefully.

"The trees," he said. "The fire would be directly into the trees. And as thick as they are, how far would a bullet go before it hit something?" Maguire studied the bush on the river bank. He shrugged.

"Not more than fifteen or twenty yards, I suppose. It would depend on the direction."

"But the marks are there," Pennycuick persisted. "Shall we find them?"

"You don't ask for much," Maguire said, doubtfully. "And, besides, that is hardly a systematic search."

"We will live dangerously," Pennycuick said, with a wink. "Come along."

Compared with their scratching in the snow, searching the trees for bullet marks was easy. One merely waded through the snow to the nearest tree then stood for several minutes, peering intently at the trunk. Maguire found a willow twig that may have been creased by a bullet. But it was doubtful. Pennycuick, however, working to the right of the trail, found what he expected. Forty feet from the bank and fifteen feet to the right, he found a tree on which two dead branches had been notched by what was clearly the same bullet. The marks were nine feet above the ground. Pennycuick dragged over a log to prop against the tree trunk as a makeshift ladder. He climbed up to examine the marks closely. Nothing but a bullet could have made the hole. Further, the hole was splintered on the side away from the river, indicating the direction of the shot. By directing Maguire back toward the ice and by sighting through the bullet holes at him, Pennycuick established, roughly, the line the bullet had taken. The bullet had been fired from the ice, in all likelihood, passing near the first pool of blood. At that point, because the bank was a few feet higher than the surface of the ice, the bullet would have been four or five feet above the ground.

Very much pleased with himself, Pennycuick climbed down from the tree and went to examine the first blood patch more closely. Maguire joined him in the shallow pit they had dug around the blood and the two men scratched and scraped with their pointed sticks. It was Maguire who, after some minutes, dislodged a string of something he at first took to be clotted blood. But upon closer examination, rubbing the blood off with his fingers, he found a cord of tissue, two inches long.

"It looks like sinew," Pennycuick said.

"Yeah, the thin bit does. But the thicker part is bone. I'd say it is a piece of skull."

"Why do you say that?"

"Just the shape of it." Maguire stood, sobered and folded the tissue in a bit of paper. He put the package in his pocket, then scooped up a handful of snow to clean his hands. "Have you got all the measurements you need for today?" he asked. Pennycuick nodded. "Then let's call it quits. I have had enough for one day."

On 24 March, the men were back on the trails, continuing the search. If the fruitless hunting of bush trails around the Arctic Express cabin had been tedious, at least walking had kept the men warm. But the minute search that was required, now that they knew where to look, was bone-chilling. Hunched in a trench in the snow, almost motionless, usually bare-handed, the men were half-frozen most of the time, in spite of the growing warmth of the sun. The sun itself was a mixed blessing. Certainly, its warmth was something to be grateful for, and the fact that the snow was being softened and settling as a result, made trails easier to locate. But, the two men knew that, as the snow melted, any evidence left in the drifts would merge in a single layer on the ground. It would no longer be possible to associate an article with a specific layer of snow and, thereby, with a rough date.

So, Maguire and Pennycuick scraped at the snow in the shoveled trench until they could stand it no longer. Then, on numb feet, they would stumble away, beating arms against their sides, to search more trees for bullet marks, or to hunt around the tent-cabin. And, when their joints ceased aching and their toes began to smart with the renewed blood supply, they came back to crawl and scratch in the snow and brush of the trail once again. It was more for the warming exercise than anything else that they shoveled the trail from the blazed tree to the dead end at the cutbank. The entire stretch yielded not a single piece of evidence but it offered a welcome change from crouching.

As time passed, however, it became more and more obvious that any evidence to be found would be found around the cabin and on the trail where the blood was. And slowly the collection of articles — some vitally important, some totally irrelevant — grew.

On 24 March, they found a garter. It was capable of holding up just about any kind of sock and could have belonged to any one of thousands of people. It lay at the correct level in the snow and that was as much as could be said about it. But, on the same day, Pennycuick found a small wad of paper in the wiry tangle of a willow bush. When he unfolded it, he saw it was a receipt. It read "Monday Dec 22nd 1899 Received L. Olsen $6 for meals and bunk J. Fussell".

The receipt was sixty feet from the bank and to the left of the trail, placing it in the welter of blood spots they had found the day before. It suggested that Olsen, the telegraph lineman, was the man who had been so hard to kill. On 25 March, Maguire found a piece of cotton rope. Its significance was uncertain. Later that same day, the men each found an empty .40-82 cartridge near the river bank. Now, it was clear that at least three shots had been fired, probably from the same rifle, and the location of the shells strengthened the notion that the three men had been driven off the river and killed by gunfire directed toward the trees. Maguire remained certain a .30-30 shell would be found.

On 26 March, Pennycuick and Maguire walked to Fussell's roadhouse at Minto. Their avowed intention was to see if the captain could identify the lime-juice bottle that Maguire had found near the tent-cabin. It was significant, however, that the trip permitted them to warm and dry themselves in the relatively sumptuous surroundings of the roadhouse and to eat a meal which would be a change from their own camp cooking.

As to Fussell's identification of the bottle, there was a pleasant surprise. John Fussell had, indeed, started the winter with a case of lime juice of that brand. He had dispensed Canadian Club whiskey in the empty bottles. He had sold such a bottle full of whiskey to Olsen. And Fussell's corkscrew, a somewhat unusual affair with a flat spiral, fitted the hole already in the cork. Captain Fussell would be a useful witness.

On 27 March, Pennycuick left for Selkirk to fetch soldiers to begin clearing the ice below the cutbank in the hope of finding bodies. On the same day, Maguire searched the area in which they believed Olsen had fallen. He found a one-dollar bill, Dominion of Canada No.388870. Then, in the same area, sixty-four feet from the bank and five feet six inches to the left of the trail, he found a bone button, one-half of a pocket comb and three cigars. Again, the items were at the correct level in the snow and they were certainly suggestive of pocket-rifling. But, the items would never be connected to any one specific person. For the next three days, Maguire toiled in the snow. He found nothing.

On 31 March, Pennycuick returned with three men of the Yukon Field Force. He had the soldiers move all the gear from the Arctic Express cabin and set up a new camp near the Pork Trail. While the soldiers were thus engaged, Pennycuick and Maguire went back to the trail. As they continued to search the area in which Olsen apparently went down, they found more articles. Sixty feet six inches up the trail and eleven feet to the right, they found two black buttons and a short piece of hemp rope. Again, it was the kind of discovery at which the men could only shrug their shoulders and record the findings in the interest of completeness. At the same spot, however, they found a medicine bottle. By the label, the bottle was Olsen's. In the same general area, but to the left of the trail, they found two more empty cartridges. The discovery cheered Maguire considerably for, while the cartridges were not .30-30s, neither were they .40-82s. They were from a .41 caliber revolver, the same caliber O'Brien carried.

Then, picking through the twigs and snow and clotted blood that lay forty feet up the trail, Pennycuick found a tooth. It was obviously a human tooth, or rather, the crown of a tooth, neatly broken off. There was no longer any doubt that the second pool of blood was human blood. They found a chunk of copper ore and a safety pin near Olsen's receipt but there was no hope of either item being useful evidence.

On 1 April, Pennycuick completed a set of maps of the search area and, with Maguire dragging the chain, measured all trails, and recorded the distances. While they were working around the tent-cabin, they found the remains of a fire to one side of the door. When they cleared the snow, they found the patch of ashes and debris to be four feet across and, on examination of the rubble, it was obvious that clothes had been burned here, too. There were bits of charred cloth, fragments of suspenders, and more eyelets.

Later that day, they found yet another empty .40-82 cartridge. A few minutes after that, while picking over the bloody mess in which the tooth had been found, Pennycuick found a smaller bit of tooth. This fragment had a bright gray smear on it, suggesting it had been struck by a bullet.

"I guess that settles it," Maguire said. "Two head shots. Fairly tricky if the men were moving at all."

"I should say it is no trick at all," Pennycuick retorted. "The range is nearly point-blank."

"Exactly. But who has his rifle sighted in at sixty feet? Nobody I ever heard of. Far more likely to be sighted in at fifty yards or a hundred yards. So, it'd be throwing high at close range. I don't suppose you tried the rifle Ryan found in the cabin to see how it shoots." Pennycuick shook his head.

"No, I did not. But, I do not believe it is important because your theory does not stand scrutiny."

"Oh? Why not?"

"Too many shots. For the thing to have been done as you describe, there would only be three shots. And they would have to be closely spaced because, as soon as the first was fired, the men who had not been hit would be warned. The firing would, therefore, have to be faster than the men could react.

"Yet we have cartridges scattered over forty or fifty feet. That means the rifleman was moving, too, and that surely makes the venture even trickier."

"But, what about the holes in the branches? They line up with the first patch of blood."

"True. But I have given that some thought. And the more I think about it, the more difficult it is to believe that one bullet made the holes in the branches after having passed through a skull. The line is simply too good. I can imagine ways the bullet might have passed through a body without striking a large bone. In such a case, it could easily stay on its original line. But, there is no easy way through a skull and a bullet, if it emerged at all, would be more likely to be off on a tangent than to be on the original line."

"Wait up, now, this is a rifle bullet we are talking about. It would have enough power to blast its way through; skull bone would hardly slow it down."

"No, I do not think so." Pennycuick was adamant. "The bullet is likely to be deflected no matter how much power is driving it. Indeed, the bullet may not even emerge — it would certainly mushroom to some extent. And depending on what it hit, it may break into fragments and not exit at all."

"All right," Maguire said, impatiently. "I grant you all that. But what is the point of your speculation anyway?"

"I am simply trying to reconstruct what happened here. I am coming to believe that the teeth and bone splinter came, not from the first shot, but from a second shot. A coup de grace, so to speak."

"A what?"

"Coup de grace: the killing stroke that ensures the death of a wounded man — a man wounded by a volley of rifle fire, for example." Maguire thought about this and, as the ugliness of the scene became clear, he grimaced.

"You mean, just walk up to a fallen man and blast him in the face?"

"Roughly, yes."

"Good grief!" Maguire said. He sighed, frowning, then he nodded slowly. "Yes," he said. "That fits the blood pools all right. All except for the mess that Olsen left. What do you reckon happened to him?"

"I do not know. It looks as if he put up a fight but that is scarcely a profound observation."

"No, it's not," Maguire said. "But, you know something? This killing shot of yours should have left a bullet in the pool of blood, shouldn't it?"

"Yes, it should. Provided of course that the bullet exited and did not disintegrate ..."

"Yeah, yeah. I heard you the first time. I'm going to have a dig in this stinking mess anyway." Maguire crouched by the blood in which the tooth had been found. Pennycuick walked to the blood nearer the bank and began to dig.

It was the work of a few minutes for Maguire to scratch through the twigs and blood to the underlying snow. It was obvious that these few inches of snow had not been penetrated and there was no bullet in the bloody slush. He rose to point out the error of Pennycuick's thinking and nearly bumped into him. The constable stood, smiling proudly, displaying a twisted lump of lead between his thumb and forefinger.

"Well, I'll be ..." Maguire said. "Where was it?"

"In the center of the pool of blood and about half an inch into the dirt."

"Caliber?" Maguire asked. Pennycuick shrugged.

"What would you say?"

"Pretty big, but it's impossible to say, what with the slug all smashed up like that. Could be a .40-82, I guess."

"It could be," Pennycuick said. "Or a .41 Colt's."

So the search continued. On 2 April, the soldiers began cutting ice at the foot of the cutbank. Pennycuick, with an improvised water glass, peered into the icy water for bodies. It took the soldiers several hours to open a strip of water. Pennycuick examined the strip in ten minutes then returned to the trail while the ice cutters opened another bit of river.

On 7 April, Maguire found another receipt. This one, as well, was made out to Olsen and had been issued from the Beef Cache roadhouse. On 8 April, they uncovered more buttons outside the tent. On 12 April, Maguire and Pennycuick made their way along the line of sight connecting the old camp with the junction of Powell's trail and the main trail. They found twenty-seven trees that had been cut down to give a clear view. All of them had been cut with the same nicked axe that had been used to cut the cabin logs and to brush out the trails. Pennycuick chopped parts of several of the trees to be used in evidence. He also took samples of the cabin logs and, for contrast, several pieces from near the telegraph line. These logs had been cut by a different axe and a different axeman, a fact readily seen when the cut surfaces were compared.

On 17 April, as they searched away from the tent in circles of increasing radius, Maguire and Pennycuick found two more buckles, another three-bladed pocket knife, and a dog chain. There was a bottle of Eclectic Oil and part of a Dr. Sandon's Electric Belt widely advertised "for any man suffering from nervous debility, varicocele, drains, and lack of vigor, etc."

That same day, Maguire at last found the .30-30 cartridge he had sought so long. Because it lay fifty feet from the cabin, however, there was no obvious way to tie the cartridge to the site of the murders. To confuse matters further, Maguire found a spent slug sixty feet from the cabin. The bullet was somewhat mushroomed but Maguire was sure it was a .30-30 soft-point. It was tempting to think that the bullet had been fired down at the river and had, by odd coincidence, fallen near the cabin. But there was no evidence whatever to support this. Finally, thirty feet from the cabin, Pennycuick found a key. It was manufactured by the E. C. Morris Safe Company of Boston and was stamped '2L7'.

The ice-cutting venture which had begun early in April had, after almost three weeks, produced no evidence. The men of the Yukon Field Force worked willingly, cutting tons of ice along a sand bar that was known to be just off the cutbank. Pennycuick's idea had been that the bodies had been caught on the bar and not swept downstream. It soon became apparent, however, that cutting ice was far too slow to allow the bar to be completely searched. In one last effort to open a large hole, one of the soldiers planted a sizable charge of dynamite in the ice. The charge produced an impressive thump which jarred bits of melting snow off the nearest spruce trees and hurled an immense quantity of shattered ice into the air. Chips and chunks of ice, some half the size of a man's head, showered down for several seconds. But, when everything had settled, the men were disappointed at the hole they had made. One of the soldiers claimed he could spit across it without even bracing himself, then proceeded to do just that. All ice-cutting was stopped on 19 April.

For the next ten days, Maguire and Pennycuick continued to search the trails. They went over ground that had been searched several times before but, because the snow was rapidly disappearing, and patches of bare ground could be seen, they thought it worthwhile to see what had been missed in the snow. On 2 May, Pennycuick found one more empty .40-82 cartridge, this one on the ice near the main trail. On 4 May, he found another key near the tent-cabin. The key was for a Yale lock and it was stamped with the code '5 L.U. 12'.

Maguire and Pennycuick then took stock of what had been found, to be sure everything was recorded. They measured the distances between several more points, checked others to be certain that the map entries were correct. Once the snow had completely melted, many features of the landscape would be gone, impossible to reconstruct. Satisfied that the maps and records were as nearly complete as they could be made, the two men ended their search, ended almost three months of hunting that had uncovered miles of tracks, hundreds of footprints, and three large patches of blood.

11
Bodies Surface

At Selkirk, the ice was gone from the river by the middle of May. Pennycuick was sure that with the ice gone the bodies would soon appear. Even Maguire, after having tramped the bush one last time now that the snow cover had melted, reluctantly agreed that the men were in the river. As a result, every policeman downstream from Minto was on the lookout for bodies. Dozens of hours were spent checking sandbars, islands, sloughs — every place a body might wash up. But, in spite of their effort, not a single body was discovered by a policeman.

On 30 May, a man reported to Corporal McPhail at Selkirk. There was a body, he said, on a bar a mile and a half upstream. McPhail sent Pennycuick to recover the body. It lay on its right side in four inches of water. There were felt boots on the feet of the corpse and, on the boot soles were marks which looked very like those made by the pedals of a bicycle. A yellow sweater was pulled up and over the head; braces dangled, fastened only at the rear. Pennycuick loaded the body in his boat and returned to Selkirk. The body was already somewhat decomposed and could be expected to deteriorate rapidly in the warm weather. It was vital, therefore, that a preliminary examination be made — Dr. Madore was at hand — and the clothing salvaged for later identification.

Early next morning, Corporal McPhail and Dr. Madore watched as Pennycuick cut the clothes from the body. He removed a silk handkerchief from around the neck and the felt boots and socks from the feet. He cut off a pair of knicker-bockers, a shirt, the yellow sweater and underclothes — a shirt and drawers — made of goatskin. The pockets yielded a door key, a bicycle wrench, and several sodden matches. Dr. Madore made a quick examination of the body and satisfied himself that all wounds were gunshot wounds, either entrance or exit. Pennycuick packed the clothes and took them and the body to Dawson for the Coroner's Inquest and autopsy.

On 8 June, Corporal McPhail again received word of a floating body. Three travelers had sighted this one at Hell's Gate, eleven miles up from Selkirk. When McPhail, Corporal Hales, and Maguire finally found the body on 11 June, it was tied to an overhanging tree where the travelers had left it. A blue sweater was pulled up and over the head; the suspenders were loose and hanging. As with the first body, Dr. Madore made a quick examination at Selkirk and shipped the corpse to Dawson. For the most urgent possible reason, the body was packed in ice. During his search of the clothing McPhail found a watch which was stopped at 9:05, a watch chain, a pin from the Yukon Order of Pioneers, part of a letter, a notebook, two pencils and six visiting cards. The name on the cards was Lynn Wallace Relfe.

On 14 June, three men sat at a rough table at the NWMP barracks in Dawson. They were Dr. William Thompson, Police Surgeon, Dr. Howard Hurdman, practicing physician, and Inspector William Scarth. Hurdman had only just arrived and was sipping a cup of tea before beginning the job at hand.

"So, we have the second one, have we?" he said, blowing on his steaming cup. " 'The Yukon yields up her dead,' if I may quote the *Daily News.*"

"Wretched rag," Thompson growled. "But, yes, we have the second. And from the smell of this one, I am not at all certain I want to see the third. You can almost see the body decompose." Scarth breathed deeply, twice, and sipped cautiously at his tea.

"Yes, that is to be expected," Hurdman said. "It is the rule with submerged bodies that decomposition accelerates once they are removed from the water. This one is Relfe, is that correct?"

"Yes," Scarth said. "Did you know him?"

"Never met the man," Hurdman replied.

"Our report states that he was shot . . ."

"Never mind that," Hurdman said, waving Scarth aside. "I will draw my own conclusions, if you don't mind." He turned again to Thompson. "Is the body in the blacksmith shed — or whatever it is — like the first one was?"

"Yes, I took . . ."

"I hope the light is better in there this time. It is most difficult to do a proper job when one has to rush outside to see what one has removed."

"I have seen to it, Doctor," Scarth said. "We removed the boards from the south window. You should have good light."

"Mm, I hope so."

At that moment, there was a rap at the door and Corporal Christopher Reid came in. He stopped, at attention, until Scarth beckoned him into the room.

"Ah, Corporal Reid," Hurdman said. "We have been waiting for you. Some tea before we start?"

"No, thank you, sir."

"Cigar, then?" he asked, offering an open silver case around the group. "You might find it useful if you think the smell of the body will be too much."

"No, thank you, sir," said Reid.

"It won't be necessary, thank you," said Scarth uncertainly. Hurdman shrugged and snapped the case closed.

"As you wish," he said. "Shall we get started?" And he led the way across the barracks yard to the shed.

Inside, on a plank table, lay Relfe's body, covered with a sheet. In the close confines of the shed, heated by the June sun, the smell was all but overpowering. Scarth steeled himself, breathed deeply, and stepped in.

"You will take my dictation, Corporal Reid, just as before," Hurdman said, rolling his sleeves.

"Yes, sir," said Reid.

"Good man. Now, to work." He whipped the sheet off the body and studied it in silence for a minute.

"The body," he began, "is that of a white male adult, about six feet tall. Weight is about one hundred sixty pounds. Appears well-nourished. The scalp and face are extensively abraded. The epidermis is absent over most of the head; muscular tissue can be seen. Head hair is absent, except for a tuft beneath the occipital cone." Hurdman turned to Inspector Scarth. "You see, Inspector, this is what I was trying to show you with the first body. It is much more apparent in this one. Bodies float face down and, because the head is slightly heavier than the rest, it rides lower. So, when the body is pushed about by the currents, the head is the part most scuffed along the river bottom. And the backs of the hands, too, incidentally. See here." Hurdman lifted the left hand of the corpse and pointed to the knuckles. The flesh was sodden, gray and deeply wrinkled.

"Now that 'washerwoman' appearance is typical of the immersed body, as I said before," Hurdman went on. "But, see there? The top skin has been stripped away through contact with the sand.

On the palm, the wrinkling is even more pronounced, but the skin is intact." He looked up questioningly at Scarth, who nodded brusquely and stepped back again, still breathing in short puffs.

"All right, then, we will carry on," Hurdman said. He reverted to his dictation voice, more precise, more resonant, for Reid's benefit.

"There is a circular wound approximately one-half inch in diameter, one inch below and one inch behind the right ear. It has the appearance of a gunshot wound. There is a second wound in the head, roughly circular, approximately one inch in its greatest dimension. This wound lies approximately one and one-half inches in front of the angle of the left jaw." Hurdman turned to a wooden tray which held his instruments and selected a ten-inch steel probe. It looked like a knitting needle. He inserted the probe in the wound behind the right ear and pressed gently. There was a momentary hesitation as the rod hit a minor obstruction, then it slid smoothly through the skull. It emerged from the hole in the left jaw, pushing ahead of it small bits of tissue and a trickle of fluid. "There is complete connection between the two wounds." Hurdman dictated.

When the probe passed, Scarth was fixated with horror. He had seen corpses, of course, and had witnessed several autopsies, including the one performed on Clayson the week before. But, while he could appreciate the necessity of the procedures, he did not have to enjoy them. Scarth breathed more quickly.

Hurdman turned slowly to the policeman. "Listen," he said. "There are two ways for you to handle this. Either take a cigar and try to drown the smell — and it has never worked for me, by the way; or you dive right in, embrace the smell, and breathe deeply through your nose. The sense of smell fatigues quickly. Look upon the body with the same detachment you would have for a haunch of rotten beef — I am sure you have had some experience with that. This body is not a man; it is only the remains; the man is gone. And on these rather foul remains we will make observations as dispassionately as possible and we will then dispose of the remains in a decent — and speedy — fashion.

"Now, choose one course or the other. But I do not want you standing there gawping like a beached fish waiting for the most inopportune time to come crashing down on my work."

Hurdman turned to Reid. "Now, Corporal. Where was I?"

"You said the wounds connected, sir."

"Ah, yes, so they did." Then, dictating again, he went on.

"The wound on the right side of the head shows a smooth margin consistent with its being a wound of entrance. The other shows a ragged, irregular margin consistent with being a wound of exit. The wounds were made by a single ball, as opposed to a charge of shot. The ball would have been greater than one-third of an inch in diameter.

"There is a mark on the neck passing horizontally below the larynx. This appears to have been caused by a rope or a band of some sort. There is a wound on the left chest, two inches below the clavicle. Superficial." Hurdman passed quickly down both arms, twisting them to examine all sides.

"Excoriation inside of left forearm," he said. "Superficial. There is a wound on the chest, five inches below the left nipple. The wound is circular and approximately one inch in diameter." He rolled the body onto the right side.

"There is a second wound," he dictated, "a counter-opening in the back, in the lumbar region." Hurdman returned the body to its original position and peered closely at the chest wound.

"There is a second wound on the chest. It lies seven inches below the left nipple. It is superficial." He swiftly examined the body, finding nothing of note.

"All right," he said. "We will open him now. I suggest we open the chest first, Dr. Thompson, if you agree." Hurdman turned to Scarth. "Are you still with us, Inspector?" he asked. Scarth nodded. Deep breathing had helped and, while he did not appear exactly robust, his nausea was diminished.

"Good," said Hurdman and turned to assist Thompson in opening the body.

Quick, precise cuts opened a Y-shaped incision, the arms of the Y starting at the ends of the collarbone and joining at the lower tip of the breastbone. The tail of the Y extended to the pubic region. Three minutes work with bone shears clipped the ribs, permitting the breastbone to be lifted away in a piece.

"Are you ready, Corporal?" Hurdman asked. Reid nodded.

"Grossly, the right lung appears normal; the left lung is collapsed and displaced toward the back of the cavity. The heart is in the proper position; there is a wound in the left ventricle; one-half inch from the apex." Hurdman made several deft cuts, freeing the heart and lungs.

"Do you see those black bits, Inspector?" he asked, pointing to the lungs. "That is carbon. You find it in people who live in large cities. And this hole in the heart is the track of the bullet which made the hole in the chest." Scarth, by this time, was more at ease and beginning to take an interest in the proceedings.

"That must be a fatal wound," he said.

"No doubt about it," Hurdman stated. "And I daresay we will find the liver has been touched, too." He set the heart and lungs aside in a pan and returned to the body.

"Yes, see here," he said. "We have a bit of a mess here but what happened is clear, I think. The bullet entered the chest, passed through the heart, the diaphragm, clipped the left lobe of the liver — just there — and struck the spleen." He removed the abdominal organs and handed them to Thompson who placed them in pans.

"Now, if you look here, you see the inside surface of the wound in the back. The bullet struck a rib. Let me see, it is the eleventh . . . no, the twelfth. The bullet struck the twelfth rib — it is broken — and passed out forming that hole in the back."

"Was this wound inflicted before the head wound?" Scarth asked. Hurdman shrugged, raising his gory hands.

"There is really no way to tell," he answered. "I would guess so, but nobody wants guesses. I will say, though, that with this wound, the head wound was unnecessary; the man was already dead."

"It is of some interest to us, nonetheless," Scarth said. Hurdman looked at him puzzled for a moment, then brightened.

"Oh, yes, the tooth," he exclaimed. "Do you have it with you?" Scarth produced a paper packet containing the tooth that Maguire and Pennycuick had found in the pool of blood that lay forty feet six inches from the river bank.

"I am sorry, Inspector," Hurdman said. "I forgot about the tooth. I was so keen to see the track of the bullet through the chest and what you really wanted to see was the jaw. Why don't we open the skull now, examine that wound and check the tooth. That way, you won't have to waste any more time than necessary here."

Hurdman and Thompson set to work immediately, cutting through the scalp at the base of the skull and, at each end of the incision, extending it upward to a point just above the ear. There was a jog in the incision on the right side so the entrance wound could be left intact but, generally, the incision followed the edge of a fresh haircut. Hurdman then peeled the scalp forward until it covered the dead man's face. Scarth, who had successfully beaten back his initial discomfort, was even more at ease now: it was far easier to detach oneself from a *faceless* corpse. The policeman's new-found composure was tested, however, for Hurdman took up a short saw and, beginning at a point just above the eyebrows, carefully cut all around the skull. Scarth found this sight, and the sound of the saw, disquieting. But, as his sense of unease began to jostle for a higher position in his consciousness, the procedure was suddenly over. Hurdman took a small chisel and, with two smart raps, popped the skull cap off as he might remove the top half of a walnut shell.

"The brain is badly decomposed," Hurdman said. "But, just a moment. I will get it out of here." He severed the few bits of tissue holding the brain in place and, as he removed it, he turned the organ over and pointed to the underside.

"That dark patch there is blood," he said.

The men could now look into the empty skull — the bottom half of the walnut shell — and the extent of the damage from the gunshot wound could be easily seen.

"Now, Inspector, if you will look here," Hurdman began. "You will see, on the inside surface of the skull, around the entrance wound, an area larger than the bullet itself, in which the bone is simply shattered. There is a blasting-inward and you see this on the inside surface of an entrance wound. But, this was a large caliber weapon. Look here. The bullet came through very heavy bone but so great was the power that we have numerous fractures radiating from the hole: here, into the base of the skull, and here, and here. And look at this one. The fracture runs right across the base of the skull and up to the temporal bone on the other side.

"That same bullet, then, on its slightly downward path, struck the left jaw, breaking it up badly. And I would be astounded if it did not smash several teeth in the process. Let's have a look, shall we?" Hurdman pried the jaw open and, pressing the swollen tongue aside, peered into the mouth.

"I will have to clean some of the muck out of here so I can see what I am about," he said. Thompson helped roll the body on its left side. Hurdman swabbed the shattered mouth gently with a bit of rag on a stick.

"That is better," he said. "Corporal, be good enough to take this down. There are loose pieces in this mouth and I do not want to forget where anything is." He began to dictate.

"On the right side, upper, the teeth are intact. There is a silver filling in the first molar, a small silver filling in the second molar, the second bicuspid is a gold tooth. On the left side, upper, the second bicuspid is missing. There is a large silver filling in the first molar. The first bicuspid is a gold tooth. On the right side, lower, all teeth are intact. On the left side, lower, . . . let me see . . . the third molar is missing. The second molar is broken off and lying in the mouth. There is some attached tissue.

"I believe we have it, Inspector," said Hurdman, resuming a conversational tone. "The root of the third molar is there — you can see it easily — but the crown is gone. Now let me have that tooth." He took the tooth from the paper that Scarth held open. He probed and fitted for several minutes, now squinting in the dead man's mouth, now checking through the gaping wound in the jaw. He grunted, pried the mouth open a little farther, and tried again. At last he looked up at Scarth and grinned broadly.

"You have a match, Inspector," he said. "Or to be more accurate, the tooth matches the stump — perfectly. Have a look." He straightened and, with his forefinger pressing the third molar into place, directed Scarth's attention.

"You can see that the broken surfaces coincide perfectly. At first, I thought they did not but I had the blasted tooth in backwards. But not only do the broken surfaces coincide, there are the two spots of decay which you saw on the crown. They correspond exactly to decayed bits on the stump in the jawbone. You can see one of the spots through the wound there." Scarth nodded, delighted.

"Yes, it is a perfect match. No doubt about it," he said. "My men will be overjoyed to hear this because it puts this body on the bush trail they have been searching. Thank you, Doctor Hurdman."

"You are most welcome, Inspector. Now, Dr. Thompson and I will finish if you like, and you can get some fresh air. If we find anything unexpected, we will call you." Scarth retrieved the crown, wrapped it, and replaced it in his pocket.

"How much longer do you expect to be?" he asked. Hurdman looked inquiringly at Thompson.

"Half an hour?" Thompson estimated.

"Yes" Hurdman agreed. "I think half an hour should do it."

"I will see that tea is waiting for you, gentlemen," Scarth said, and turned to leave.

"Good idea," Hurdman said. "We will also need a quantity of soap and water for washing up. And a bottle of brandy to lace the tea with would be splendid."

Finally, on 26 June, a third body was reported to Constable

Frederick Reeves at Selwyn. He went to Island Post by canoe where he found the body which had been tethered to a stump by the finder. A shirt and a sweater had apparently been pulled up and over the head but, such clothing as there was, was much tattered. So advanced was decomposition that Reeves had difficulty loading the body in his canoe; pieces of flesh would simply come away from the body if it was handled roughly. Once loaded, however, Constable Reeves solved any problems of unloading. He paddled to Stewart and there had his canoe hoisted, along with its ghastly load, aboard the steamer *Canadian.*

In Dawson, Reeves turned the entire cargo over to Corporal Ryan, put in a request for a replacement canoe and headed for the business section of Dawson. There was a place that advertised two-dollar baths and Reeves meant to have one.

On 27 June, Dr. Hurdman examined the third body. Loss of soft tissue was extensive; facial features were obliterated. Indeed all that was left of the features of Lawrence Olsen, lineman, was a grinning skull. But even that was enough: Olsen's narrow jaws and prominent teeth could be recognized. Several people who had known him were prepared to swear to the identity of the remains.

As to the manner of death, Dr. Hurdman observed a gunshot wound to the head as he had in the cases of Relfe and Clayson. But, there was no body wound in Olsen's body. What distinguished Olsen's body from the others, however, were the extensive fractures of the skull, quite apart from those caused by passage of the bullet. Hurdman concluded that Olsen had been struck a crushing blow to the head — at least one blow, maybe more — with some heavy, blunt instrument. The doctor could not be sure which had come first, the gunshot or the clubbing, since either by itself would have been fatal. He was inclined, however, to believe that the clubbing had come first with the gunshot administered for good measure. Dr. Hurdman wrote his third autopsy report for Inspector Scarth.

12
Kid West

Relfe's corpse was precisely what the police needed to establish their case. Relfe was well known in Dawson and his remains were conclusively identified by several of his friends. And the broken tooth established beyond any doubt where he had died: in the snow near the Pork Trail.

On 15 June, 1900, a coroner's jury heard the evidence of Dr. Hurdman and Dr. Thompson. The jurors found that "Lynn Wallace Relfe was murdered on or about Christmas Day by a party or parties to the jurors aforesaid unknown". The body, having supplied the crucial evidence, could, at last be decently disposed of. Relfe's friends, as a final gesture to their dead companion, contributed enough money to have the body embalmed, sealed in a metal casket, and shipped home to Seattle.

The Mounted Police now had the evidence needed to lay a murder charge and none too soon either. George O'Brien had been returned to Dawson in late March and, on the way through Selkirk, Pennycuick had identified him as the man, Miller, who was wanted for cache theft. At that time, O'Brien was suspected of having killed Clayson, Olsen, and Relfe but, as Pennycuick repeatedly said, it remained suspicion only. No case worthy of the name could be brought against George O'Brien or anyone else because there were no bodies.

Still, the suspicion was strong and the Mounted Police were intent upon holding O'Brien until the mystery of the three men's disappearance could be solved. Their means for holding him was simple: he would be charged with cache theft, the crime for which he was arrested in the beginning. Accordingly, on 2 April, he was charged with the theft of a case of marmalade. That had been enough to ensure his continued presence in Dawson until June. There was a limit, however, to the number of such charges which could legitimately be brought against O'Brien. The last of them, this one involving articles from the meat cache, was laid on 18 June. On that day, Inspector Scarth sat in the courtroom, more from idle curiosity than anything else. It made little difference what happened in these proceedings, because now the murder charge could be laid at leisure. To be sure, it would take some time to assemble witnesses and organize exhibits, but the case was solid. And Scarth found, to his amusement, that he need not have feared that O'Brien would escape police clutches.

He watched as George O'Brien stood to hear the charge read. Judge Dugas frowned at the sheet of paper in his hands, then peered at O'Brien over his spectacles.

"You have heard the charge," he said. "How do you plead? Guilty or not guilty."

"Not guilty."

"Be seated."

Herbert Robertson, who was acting in O'Brien's defense, nodded to his client to sit down. Then he turned to the bench.

"My Lord, I respectfully submit that, in all fairness to my client a trial date should be set as early as possible in this matter. He has been in custody some six months now and has suffered delay after delay . . ."

"It will be quite the contrary, Mr. Robertson," the judge said. "I may as well say plainly that the prisoner is under suspicion upon some grave charges and he will be held until those charges can be thoroughly investigated."

"But, my Lord, with all respect, my client has a right to know the charges against him — all the charges. And he has the right to answer those charges."

"Indeed he does — yes, he *certainly* does. But he does not have the right to expect any zeal on the part of this court in the matter of his trial. He will wait his turn."

Scarth left the courtroom feeling more satisfied than he had in a long time. The judge's decision, in Scarth's mind at least, gave approval to police suspicions. Whatever case they had might fail because of inadequate evidence but it would not fail because the only suspect had been allowed to go free.

The same day, Scarth met with Fred Wade, the prosecutor. Two days later, George O'Brien was formally charged with the murders of Clayson, Olsen, and Relfe. This set in motion a series of events which were, in their own way, almost as demanding and frustrating as the investigation itself. There was the matter of simply locating the witnesses and somehow ensuring they would be on hand. Some would be needed for the preliminary hearing; all would be needed for the trial. Some were in Dawson and were likely to remain there. But there were others like Hildebrand, for example, the man from the steamer *Nora*, who was upstream somewhere. But nobody knew precisely where.

Hildebrand's evidence was crucial. When the police first heard of O'Brien's offer to sell the double nugget, it was obvious that such evidence could be telling. The only question at that time was whether Hildebrand would be a credible witness. Scarth had since spoken to him and was impressed with the man's forthrightness. He would be an excellent witness and his evidence would place something belonging to one of the dead men in O'Brien's hands. Hildebrand would be found.

And there were the Prathers. Scarth heard of them through Albert Gibson. The Prathers, apparently, had seen O'Brien at the Pork Trail two days after Christmas. That, too, was powerful evidence and it was desperately needed. But, if the whereabouts of Hildebrand was somewhat vague, God alone knew where the Prathers were. Scarth knew for sure only that they had gone outside. Some people in Dawson said the Prathers were going to California, others said they were going east. But nobody really knew. The main hope was a persistent rumor that the Prathers would be back, probably heading for Nome. So, the Mounted Police kept close watch on the passenger lists on the steamships and waited, hoping to intercept the Prathers on their way through Dawson. There was nothing else to do.

Locating all the witnesses was simple police work, requiring only time. But in that lay a dilemma: the later O'Brien's trial date, the better the chances of finding witnesses like the Prathers, but the more likely it would be that witnesses already located would become scattered. It was, Scarth felt, much like holding a fistful of quicksilver. One day the police would know where most of their witnesses were; the next day, someone would be off to the creeks, someone else would be going to Skagway, someone else would be going freighting. Keeping track of everyone was the Devil's own job and the longer the delay, the worse it would become.

Nor was that all Scarth had to worry about. He was plagued by a particularly difficult and distasteful problem named George West. This man first became known to Scarth through an article in the *Seattle Post-Intelligencer* of 14 April in which it was claimed that West possessed evidence important to the suspected murders. From the beginning, Scarth doubted the value of anything West had to say because the man was obviously untrustworthy. He told his story from the jail in Seattle, a fact which said as much about West as Scarth cared to know. And this was not his only time in jail, either; it was but the last of a long series of arrests for a man who was, at various times, George West, The Clear Kid, Kid West, George Wesler, and Mr. Webb.

Whatever Scarth's misgivings, however, he had no choice but to deal with Kid West because, while the police were secretive about their findings in the investigation, West was not at all reluctant to tell what he knew — or claimed to know — to any reporter who would listen. And there was no shortage of reporters willing to print the stories. In a matter of days, countless versions of what George West had said were circulated and people developed their own certainties. They were certain that the solution to the Yukon mysteries was to be found in Seattle. They knew that the police had said little about their investigation, probably because all their work had been for nothing. People *knew* that West had helped with the murders of Clayson, Olsen and Relfe or that he had been an eyewitness to the crime or that he had helped O'Brien escape or that he had heard O'Brien confess the crime. It made no difference that many of the stories did not correspond with known facts or that the stories were not even consistent with one another. What was important was that Kid West's story was in the newspapers and Scarth could not ignore them.

Thus, in the spring of 1900, when Scarth needed every available policeman in the Yukon, he sent Constable Seely to Seattle to talk to Kid West and find out exactly what testimony he was prepared to give. What Seely found in the person of George West was not encouraging. West had once been called a lying little blowhard and Seely could only agree. In fact, much later, the *Daily Klondike Nugget* would call Kid West "that synonym of monumental untruthfulness". But, in the spring of 1900, opinion was widespread that West's evidence would solve the O'Brien mystery at a stroke. So, Seely persevered.

He found that West would testify that, in January or February of 1899, O'Brien had offered him the chance to be a partner in a money-making venture. The plan was to hold up travelers on the trail, kill them, and put the bodies under the ice: a perfect crime if ever there was one. West, of course, turned down the opportunity but he was now interested that justice be done. His testimony would cost five hundred dollars.

As Seely expected, West's story was far less spectacular than the newspaper reports had it. West was not an eyewitness, he had heard no confession, he had not even seen O'Brien in more than a year. Still, the story was strong evidence, suggesting that O'Brien had planned his crime for months. It would be a compelling revelation — if anyone could believe Kid West.

As he pondered West's statement, Seely understood that he had no choice but to take the man to Dawson, even though he suspected the story was pure fabrication. There was nothing in the story that had not been suggested and discussed at length in the newspapers, except for West's assertion that O'Brien had offered him a partnership. But the story could not be proven false and at least one point, that West and O'Brien had served time together on the Dawson woodpile, was supported by prison records.

The key point, however, was the offer of partnership, and the only evidence of that came from the lips of Kid West. There could be no hope of corroboration; the value of the testimony depended heavily upon the credibility of the witness. And Kid West lied about everything, including his own name. He would, Seely was sure, be a disastrous witness. But Scarth and Fred Wade would make the decision. Arrangements were made to transport Kid West to Dawson when he was needed.

When Scarth received Seely's report, he recognized the problem: to risk weakening the Crown's case by using an unreliable witness or to risk the accusation that evidence had been withheld by not calling him. But, as much as the problem nagged at him, Scarth knew what the decision would be: West would be called to testify, no matter what. Justice would be seen to be done.

After some delays, O'Brien's preliminary hearing was held in the summer of 1900 and he was committed for trial in June 1901. In the months between, Scarth and his men checked and recorded the dozens of details that made up their case against George O'Brien. Many of the points were minor but every scrap of evidence that could be used was checked.

For example, from the first, Pennycuick claimed that the stove in Miller's camp at Hell's Gate and the stove in the tent-cabin were one and the same. This opinion was based largely on the peculiarities of the damper on the stove. As corroboration, the police found not one, but three, Dawson tinsmiths who were willing to state that, in their experience too, the damper arrangement was un-usual.

The samples of red slush from the murder trail looked to the police like blood. So did the stain on O'Brien's sled. But, an opinion which carried greater weight would be useful. So Gustav Beraud, assayer and chemist, was asked to examine the exhibits and give his conclusions. Beraud was a careful man who would not be hurried in his examination. Neither would he yield to the temptation to draw more significant conclusions than his analysis warranted. After much deliberation, he concluded that all the specimens contained blood. He was careful to point out that he could not tell whether the blood was from a horse, a dog, an ox or a human being, but he was certain it was blood.

Constables Edward McBeth and Anson Lynn would identify the double-bit axe with the nicked blade as belonging to George O'Brien. They had recaptured him after his escape from jail in the winter of 1898 and the axe, they claimed, was part of his kit at the time. Supporting evidence would, no doubt, be found in the police records of prisoners' effects.

And there were the dozens of items which Pennycuick and Maguire dug out of the snow near the Pork Trail. Some of the articles, such as the cartridge cases and Olsen's receipt, were useful evidence from the instant they were found. Others, such as the bit of rope and the garter, were so much rubbish, unidentifiable and worthless as evidence. But a few items were transformed as if by magic from pieces of trash to strong evidence.

Will Clayson would identify the pocket knife with the chipped blade as his brother's. It was a bowling prize. He would further be able to show — to Pennycuick's great delight — that the keys marked "5L.U.12" and "2L7" fitted drawers in the Clayson business safe in Skagway. Will Clayson was eager to see his brother's murderer punished. He would definitely testify and he would bring the drawers for demonstration in court.

Corporal Patrick Ryan was detailed to photograph all structures and trails near Powell's Pork Trail. In due course, James Hildebrand was found. *He* knew he wasn't lost. Jennie Prather was intercepted on her way through Dawson: police patience had paid off. She had steamship passage booked for Nome and, over her most vigorous objections, she was detained, interviewed, and served with a subpoena ordering her to appear at the trial. Her husband, however, eluded the welcoming committee of Mounted Policemen and escaped to Nome in a small boat.

While this was going on, Scarth had been able to dismiss Kid West from his mind. But the decision had been made to bring West to Dawson and, in March 1901, he arrived, under escort. And from the moment he arrived, he bombarded Scarth with a neverending stream of requests and complaints. He clearly had a high estimate of his value to the police.

He wrote:

My reasons for wanting to have some thing to Protect my self

1st When I agreed to come to Dawson over one year ago and do what I said I would, it was an under stood fact that I would Be out inside of a few months, after I agreed to come I was held at Seattle untill Dec 3 1900 7 seven months after I agreed to come. I was taken to Victoria BC Dec 3 1900, and was told that I would leave in 3 Days or on the forst Boat. I was there over 3 three months and Got near starved. I could not get a Doctor or medicine or write to any Body.

2nd Before I agreed to come to Dawson I was told that I would be treated like a white man and not Be in Iorns left Seattle Handcuffed, had Shackels on in State Room of Boat agoing to Vancouver BC, agoing to New Westminster in street car was Handcuffed Both ways. at White Horse I was Put in shackels all night in a cell at the Gaurd Room. after I left White Horse I had shackles on in Road House full of People. So you see Ive got a good Reason to want to Protect my self.

3rd Mr. Seeley said that Every thing would Be all right when I got hear. that what what he said Before. I supposed when we left Seattle he would have some thing to say about the way I would Be treated acoming in. the night I left Victoria he interduced Corpral Tredgeld like this Well Kid this is your Boss now I cant do a thing as it has Been taken out of my hands But every thing will Be all right when we Get to Dawson and he was right he did not have as much to do with me as a stranger had and If I did not tell him what I thought of the way I was ageting treated I Guess I would of Been in Iorns all the way. of course you will say it could not be helped Because I was so long ageting hear. I will admit that and I dont Blame no body for it. But I do Blame some Body for telling me one thing and adoing another. So you see by the above just how Ive Been ageting it for over a year. I tried to Get some Kind of and understanding with Mr. Seeley But he said he could Do nothing.

You Know all the Edivence in the case and just what is what and I Know Just about what Kind of a Defence will Be made and I will say this I can Break his Edivence Down If I say what he told me and state the Proposition that was made to me and a few other minor things. I would like to have an interview Before the trial so I could have a little time to Get every thing streight also to see what you thought of the Edivence you could see if it was all right If you want to Know just what I agreed to do I will let you Know at the first oppurnity. But it has Got to Be Privet as I Dont want no Body But you to Know what I am aDoing. Hpoeing you will Consider this I

reamane yours Respectfully

KID WEST

PS what ever Passes between us will Be Held secret I will Give my word of Honor on it. expect the same from you.

After his initial interview with West, Seely had told Scarth what he thought was prompting the Kid to offer testimony: the five hundred dollar fee, which was ludicrous, but also the long trip to Dawson and the chance for escape along the way. Seely felt sure that West would forget about the money — a long shot proposition, anyway — and run the first chance he got. Whatever else came of West's trip, Seely said, he must not escape. Recognizing how embarrassing it would be for the Mounted Police to lose a prisoner on loan from the Americans, Scarth agreed. Kid West might run, but his style and speed would be severely hampered — by irons.

But if Kid West was given no chance to escape, he seemed to be undaunted by the fact. He still had winning cards to play. On 17 May 1901, he wrote to Scarth asking that a friend be permitted to visit the jail. In the letter, he noted that his friend knew Ed Cudher, the sheriff in Seattle, and if the permit was not issued "she is lible to write a Big letter to Seattle and say I am ageing Ill treated and Ed Cudher will Publish the letter and I dont want no more News Paper notirary". West could not have chosen an approach less likely to succeed. He could not know precisely how poor his reputation was with Inspector Scarth but he had had some experience with the Mounted Police months before. He ought to have known that any attempts to gain advantage through threats were doomed.

But, on 29 May, West wrote again, still trying to make a deal:

I suppose Mr Seely told you what I agreed to do But I want some thing to insure me agenst ageting the worst of it. Before I take the stand. as yet Ive Got nothing only what the Seattle officials told me and that dont Go hear. My intentions are to Do what is right to the officials hear But I want to protect my self at the same time. Hopeing this will Be sadsifectory I reamane yours Respectfulley
   Geo West
PS Could you fix it so I could Get my teeth fixed they Bother me a lot now.

By 7 June, Kid West had seen no progress in his situation and he was becoming shrill:

I was talking to that party this am and Constable Conors seen me acoming out of a cell and he locked me up and I told him I was Permitted to Go in a cell on Bisness. he said he did not care I would not Go in while he was on Duty no matter what was Permitted. so that look very funny to me. I think By the way things are agoing that I am ageting the worst of it Hopeing you will look in to this I reamane yrs., Resp.
   Kid West

West's feeling that he was being ignored by Inspector Scarth was perfectly accurate. With the trial but three days away, Scarth had many important details to think about. Kid West merited no attention at all. He was securely in jail; he was one witness who would not disappear.

Besides that, there had been another development which reduced the value of West's stock even further. The Mounted Police had found yet another witness: Chris Williams. He would testify that in May of 1898, O'Brien had offered him the same deal that Kid West claimed had been offered to *him*. The difference was that Chris Williams was a working man of apparent integrity. He would be a credible witness.

So, both men would testify; Williams because he could be believed, West because he could not be ignored. And the court would assign each man's evidence its proper weight.

Crowds gather outside the Dawson courthouse during the trial (PA-16308/Public Archives Canada)

Crowds vie for position at Dawson courthouse, June 1901 (PA-16269/Public Archives Canada)

Tuesday June 20th 1901

Captain Scarth

Sir.

Please allow me to recall a fact to your remembrance. If the police have any evidence in their possession, or witnesses (of the force) who can support my statement, let me ask you not to withhold it. The facts are these:—

Sept. 17th on discharge, I found all my outfit was lost. I went & complained to Provost Tweedy.— He told me to write out a list & I wrote out as follows:—

2 stoves	Provost Tweedy signed it as correct
2 tents —	I took it to Captain Scarth acting
1 robe —	quartermaster. He sent it to O.C.
1 axe —	Steele. who signed it & quarter-
1 blanket	master gave it to Constable E Smith
1½ sacks flour	in my presence, and Smith issued
1 " 50 lbs. beans	every article to me, except 2 stoves &
1 " " apples	he gave me an order on Shindler
1 " " bacon	for a new stove & Paddy Oaktown
1 " " potatoes	gave me another out of the quarters.
" 40 sugar	Smith & the soldier who assisted
30 coffee	him to issue stores & Oaktown
10 tea	were present & Smith found an
4 buckwheat	axe-head (single edge) with the
	handle broke off through use
	he gave me a new handle to fit
	in & remarked to Oaktown put
	this in for him.— I said that's all

Sir. right. I can fix it myself.—

Let me ask you to deal fair with me & don't let them know that Lynn & McBeth have sworn to an axe I never saw. or they will deny me justice.— respectfully your

George Ritchie

Kid West's letter to Scarth, 3 July 1901 (Public Archives Canada RG 18 vol 254 File 318 Pt 4)

Facing page: O'Brien's letter to Scarth, 20 June 1901 (Public Archives Canada RG 18 vol 254 file 318 Pt 4)

The artist's sketches of the principals appearing on these pages originated in a special edition of *The Daily Klondike Nugget,* 23 August 1901.

George O'Brien, the man who was executed

The Notorious Kid West

Justice Dugas (left) and Prosecutor Wade

Detective Maguire (left) and Constable Pennycuick

That big yellow dog, Bruce

13
The Trial

At ten minutes to ten on the morning of 10 June 1901, there was a line of people fifty yards long waiting for the doors to open to the courthouse. For the first ten yards, the line was orderly, made up of men — some accompanied by their wives — who had come early and whose place in line was not in dispute. Some stood chatting quietly, some squatted on their heels, smoking. Mrs. David Archibald sat almost regally on a simple wooden chair her husband had brought. A Mr. Wainwright, a businessman from San Francisco, was forty-first in line and, behind him, the line degenerated rapidly. What began as an orderly queue became groups of three, four or six, jostling and arguing. Places were swapped and stolen; bitter arguments ensued as to who was ahead of whom in line. One man, a determined devil in a shiny brown suit, had improved his position from about seventy-fifth to fiftieth on his ability to cut a higher card than the person ahead of him.

Inside the courthouse, Inspector Scarth was helping Fred Wade with final preparations. The exhibits, the one-hundred and fifty-odd items ranging from the dead men's clothing to a lime juice bottle to sections of tree stump were Scarth's responsibility and now he was checking and rechecking everything to be sure each item would be at hand when it was needed. All appeared to be in order.

Fred Wade hooked his thumbs in his vest pockets. "Well, Captain, is everything here?" he said.

"I think so," Scarth said.

"Good. And by the way, you won't forget to get some putty, will you? So Noble and what's-his-name — uh — Hildebrand, can make models of the nugget. No rush, just be sure it's here, will you?"

"I'll have one of the men see to it. Although we may not need it — Hildebrand has not shown up yet. I don't know what has become of him. And, I told him, too. Be here *before* ten o'clock, I said. And what does he do? Dawdle along and dawdle along."

"Ah, relax, Captain, we have plenty of time. I have already seen

Dr. Hurdman this morning. I'll be putting him on first to give the medical evidence, then McPhail and Pennycuick to describe finding the bodies, then the people who identified the bodies at the inquests. It will be three days before I have finished with them. Your stragglers have lots of time to appear."

"Mm- I suppose. But still they were *told* ..."

"Anyway, here we go ready or not. Piper has just opened the gates."

And like water through a breached dam, the crowd that had collected in the street surged into the courtroom, the ladies gamely trying to preserve some scrap of dignity as their escorts briskly propelled them toward the best seats. The men abandoned all pretense at civility and shoved and elbowed for a seat, any seat.

Fred Wade leaned toward Scarth and whispered, "Look at that mob and then tell me man is a civilized animal." Scarth smiled in reply.

Within three minutes, the courtroom was filled. Every seat was taken and all standing room was occupied, except for doorways which the police kept clear. Every window was filled with faces as those left outside stretched and gawked, trying to catch a glimpse of the proceedings. Now and then, a face would disappear and, instantly, another would pop up to take its place.

Charles McDonald, the court clerk, bustled about ensuring that the stenographer was ready, that the water pitchers were filled, that counsel for the Crown and the accused were ready to proceed. Satisfied, he went to a side door, opened it, beckoned. The babble of conversation in the courtroom ceased instantly and the attention of everyone was focused on the doorway in which stood George O'Brien and Constable Connor.

For many of the spectators, it was the first time they had seen George O'Brien, the man who was supposed to have killed so savagely. One could sense their disappointment at what they saw for George O'Brien was a very ordinary-looking man. Even Staff Graham, the stickler for precise description, would have agreed that "middling height, middling weight, medium complexion, dark hair" was the only possible description of the man. One could see expressions of bewilderment, too, expressions that betrayed the thought: "There must be some mistake — he doesn't *look* like a killer." It was a widely-held opinion that the criminal type invariably had criminal features and criminal features were easily recognized. But George O'Brien presented no striking feature. He was neatly dressed, his hair was freshly cut, he was clean-shaven. That, of course was at the insistence of his counsel, Henry Bleeker, who felt that the simplest way to convince a court that one is a ruffian is to look like a ruffian. It is much more difficult to think badly of the man who is well turned out and Bleeker wanted the jury's first impression of his client to be as favorable as possible.

O'Brien stopped at the doorway and whispered something to Connor. The policeman nodded and pointed to the prisoner's box. O'Brien stepped into the hushed courtroom and walked slowly across the floor. He was wearing black felt boots with soft soles like those on carpet slippers. But the spectators were so silent that every footstep was clearly heard. As he stepped into the prisoner's box, there was a sharp crack which caused one of the ladies in the front row to start visibly. It was only then that people noticed that O'Brien's wrists were manacled. He had accidentally struck the rail with the short loop of chain which hung between his hands. O'Brien was still standing when the clerk announced Judge Dugas. McDonald stood aside the door and bawled, "Ar-dur!"

As the crowd stood, Judge Dugas swept into the room, sat, adjusted his spectacles and opened the ledger in front of him.

"This court's now in session. Be seated," said McDonald.

The trial of George O'Brien had begun.

The court first dealt with a number of motions made by counsel for the defense. In particular, Henry Bleeker insisted that his client be tried for the murder of one man, not of all three. Judge Dugas granted the motion and Fred Wade chose to go ahead with the charge that O'Brien had murdered Lynn Wallace Relfe. This was the obvious choice because Relfe's body could be identified reliably and the broken tooth showed, beyond doubt, that he had been killed near the Pork Trial.

Olsen, on the other hand, would have been a poor choice, partly because his body had been so badly decomposed that recognition was all but impossible. But it was also a fact that few people had known him well. Indeed, at O'Brien's preliminary hearing, Olsen's first name had not been clearly established and he was recorded as " -------- Olsen." There was something sad about that. The man whose disappearance had initially triggered the investigation, the man who had defended himself so courageously was, in the end, recorded only as "--------- Olsen" because so few people knew him well enough to call him by his first name.

The fact that O'Brien would be tried only for the murder of

Relfe was no inconvenience for Fred Wade. He expected defense's motion. And he expected the motion to be granted. But, he fully intended to use evidence relating to the deaths of Clayson and Olsen, as well, whenever it suited him. He would rely on the argument that the killing of the three men was a single act and, therefore, evidence pertaining to one dead man also applied to the others. Wade knew counsel for the defense would object any time Clayson and Olsen were mentioned. But, he was also confident that those objections would not prevail. Henry Bleeker's motion had been granted but it was a hollow victory.

Counsel for the defense was not yet finished, however. He immediately moved that all charges against his client be dropped because, he claimed, evidence taken in the preliminary hearing was insufficient to support a charge of murder. The court rejected his argument, as Bleeker must have known it would. But it was always worth a try.

The remainder of that first morning was spent picking the six jurors who would hear the case. The process was quick. Twenty-four citizens had been called for jury duty. Within an hour, thirteen had been dismissed, either for cause or through peremptory challenges, a fourteenth man had begged off because of his poor eyesight, and counsel had agreed on six men: Wilfred DeLage, T. Ross Moulton, William R. King, Frank J. Dixon, Garren Reed, and Arthur F. Rolph. Those whose only experience was with American courts were astonished that a jury was chosen so quickly. In the United States, it was said, a trial of this sort might require that a thousand prospective jurors be called and selection of the jury from this group might take a week. Here, it was over by lunchtime.

One potential source of delay — the reluctance of people to serve on the jury — was eliminated by Judge Dugas at the outset. Anyone who thought of disqualifying himself from duty on some trifling grounds had better think again, the judge said. The court would not tolerate citizens who tried to sidestep their duty.

The jury, once chosen, was placed in the care of Corporal John Storm Piper and Constable David Moyne. These men were instructed by Judge Dugas that the jurors were not to leave the courthouse for the duration of the trial. This was an unpleasant surprise to at least one of the jurors who obviously had doubts about the accommodation that could be offered in the courthouse. Then, following the judge's warning that the jurors were to be allowed to speak to nobody and that they were to have no papers, court was adjourned until two o'clock.

In the afternoon, Fred Wade began the case for the Crown. In his opening remarks, he intended to present the outline of the crime as it had been reconstructed by the Mounted Police investigators. Some detail was unavoidable, but he would keep detail to a minimum because that sort of evidence was much more effective coming from individual witnesses. Besides, there were so many small points that, had he tried to tell the whole tale, there was the risk that the jurors would become confused, drowned in a bog of unconnected facts. Above all, Wade wanted to leave the jury with a simple, solid framework upon which they could build as the evidence was brought out. It was imperative that they understand the crime in general. He did, however, want two specific points to stick in the jurors' minds: the wounds found in the bodies and the facts of the strange double nugget.

As it had been in the morning, the courthouse was packed with spectators and, in the warm June sun, its temperature was rising by the minute. Already the atmosphere was muggy, thick with a mixture of sweat and perfume. Fred Wade stood, silent, apparently intent upon checking his notes. He was, in fact, checking nothing; he knew exactly what he wanted to say and how he wanted to say it. His pause — a slow count of five — was calculated to get all attention focused upon himself. He took out a spotless white handkerchief, dabbed at the moisture on his forehead, then straightened and looked directly at William R. King, the juror on the left.

"Gentlemen," he said, "we are about to enter upon the trial of a crime which, from the peculiar circumstances surrounding it, makes it the most intricate trial of the most diabolical crime probably ever committed on this continent.

"In all cases of this kind it is necessary to prove that a man has been killed before you can attempt to prove that someone killed him. I will not go into the medical evidence just at this point, but will state the facts concerning the finding of the bodies. The bodies of three men were found on a bar in the Yukon River at a point near Selkirk."

As Wade expected, Bleeker was instantly on his feet, objecting to the mention of three bodies when only one was specified in the charge. But, Wade did not expect what happened next. Judge Dugas simply looked at counsel for the defense, shook his head and said, "Proceed, Mr. Wade."

The prosecutor continued his address: "On the 28th of May, 1900, a body was discovered on a sand bar near Selkirk with two bullet holes through it and we will produce evidence to show the body to be that of Clayson.

"On June 8th, 1900, another body was found on a bar with two bullet holes through it and we will prove it to be the body of Lynn Relfe.

"On the 27th of June the body of Olsen was brought to Dawson.

"The medical evidence will show the condition of the bodies when they were discovered. The body of Relfe showed he had been shot in two places — once through the trunk and once in the head."

As he described the wounds, Wade moved a step closer to the jury and pointed to his own body, showing, roughly, the track of each bullet as he referred to it.

"Clayson," he continued, "had been dealt with in much the same way, while with Olsen the method of procedure had been somewhat different, he being clubbed to death."

At that Wade heard a slight gasp and saw, from the corner of his eye, a lady in the front row press a scrap of lace to her lips in horror. He returned his attention to the jurors and spoke more slowly, more emphatically.

"His body showed that his ribs, both in front and behind, had been broken with some heavy instrument, besides which his head had been shot into an almost unrecognizable pulp."

Wade paused again, just long enough for each juror to construct his own mental picture of Olsen's corpse. Then he carried on, describing the known movements of Clayson and Relfe, their meeting with Olsen at Fussell's roadhouse, Ryan's search for Olsen, the finding of the tent-cabin and, finally, the search of the murder trail itself. Wade had been speaking for nearly an hour. The courtroom was by now oppressively hot and he was sweating profusely. He took a sip of water and continued.

"The Crown will present evidence to show that the accused approached one man with the proposition that they rob travelers on the trail during the coming winter."

"He is a false witness!" O'Brien exclaimed. Wade carried on as if there had been no interruption.

"I will further show," he said, "that the accused also proposed to another man that they hold up and rob the mail on the upper river and murder the drivers and put their bodies into the river through the ice."

"NO!" O'Brien cried, scrambling to his feet. "They are both policemen and false witnesses." Constable Connor swiftly moved to restrain O'Brien. Judge Dugas scowled at the prisoner and sharply called for order. Henry Bleeker turned to his client, hissing at him to stay seated and quiet. The courtroom was abuzz with the muttered disapproval of the spectators.

Fred Wade stood calmly, hands clasped behind him like a preacher. He did not smile because that would have been unseemly. But O'Brien's outburst had been most satisfactory; the jurors would know that Wade had touched a nerve. They would be all the more attentive when Chris Williams took the stand.

Besides that, however, Fred Wade had enough experience with juries to know that it was practically impossible to hold their attention for much more than an hour at a stretch, no matter what sort of story they were being told or how emphatically it was presented. They needed a break in which to stretch and shift in their seats and let their minds wander to other things.

Within minutes, order was restored and Wade firmly drew the jury back to his story. He traced O'Brien's movements in the early winter of 1899, emphasizing the presence of a partner, Graves. He showed the jurors how O'Brien and Graves were slowly making their way upstream from Selkirk, robbing caches along the way. He had already traced the line of Clayson and Relfe and now he showed that the trail of O'Brien and Graves cut that line near Minto on Christmas Day, 1899.

The prosecutor admitted that after December 19, O'Brien had disappeared, not at all surprising when one considered the plan he was about to put in action. But, said Wade, when O'Brien was next seen, on December 27 at the Pork Trail, he was alone, traveling fast and he had money. All of that, however, could have been perfectly innocent but for a later event.

"We will produce evidence," Wade said, "to the effect that O'Brien stayed overnight on the steamer *Nora*. While there, he displayed a small sack of nuggets to a man named Hildebrand. One of the nuggets was a rare piece, a double nugget in which a small nugget was contained within a larger one and rattled when handled.

"The accused, upon seeing this strange nugget, hastily concealed it — you will hear evidence to that effect."

Wade was nearly done. His suit was soaked through with sweat. He mopped his face with his now-sodden handkerchief and went on, emphasizing each word with stabs of his forefinger.

"That nugget was the property of Lynn Relfe, presented to him by George Noble of Dawson." He paused briefly yet again.

"A day or two later, when O'Brien was arrested by the police in Tagish, the tell-tale nugget had disappeared and has not been seen since." With that, Fred Wade thanked the jurors and sat down, having spoken for two hours.

True to his stated plan, the prosecutor called Dr. Hurdman as the Crown's first witness. Hurdman gave excellent testimony, not cluttering his statements with technical language as so many medical men were prone to do, but giving clear evidence in plain English. Wade noted with satisfaction that the jurors were mightily impressed by the doctor's description of Relfe's wounds. The description was simple, dispassionate, and utterly ghastly.

Wade then led the doctor into a description of the autopsies of Clayson and Olsen. Once again, counsel for the defense objected and, this time, the point was argued. Judge Dugas ruled that Wade's argument was sound and that, as soon as there was proof that the three men were traveling together, evidence pertaining to Clayson and Olsen could be applied in the present case.

Having established through Dr. Hurdman's testimony that three men were, in fact, dead and that they had not drowned but had died of gunshot wounds, Wade called Corporal McPhail, Constable Pennycuick, and Constable Reeves to describe the circumstances under which the bodies had been found and how they came to be transported to Dawson.

Then came a string of witnesses who had known the dead men and who had identified their remains. Abe Ritzwaller told how he had helped Relfe prepare for the trip out of Dawson in 1899, how they had taken breakfast together on the morning of Relfe's departure, how they had walked together, chatting and joking, as Relfe began the journey. Ritzwaller positively identified the body of his friend. Murray Eads knew Lynn Relfe very well. Eads owned the Pavilion and Relfe had worked for him for over a year. There was no doubt in his mind that the body he had seen at the Barracks was that of Lynn Relfe.

And, in case there remained any doubt of the identity of the body found on 8 June 1900, Wade called Arthur Lewin. A notebook had been found in the dead man's pocket and tucked in its pages was a receipt. Lewin identified his own signature on the receipt and stated that he had given the receipt to Lynn Relfe.

In a similar fashion, Fred Wade established the identity of Clayson's body. Elmer White was a reporter who had known Clayson well and Thomas Firth had shared Clayson's cabin. Both men were positive about the identity of the body.

Finally, William Holden, the telegraph operator from Five Fingers and Olsen's boss was called. Wade showed him human jaws, with teeth still attached, which had been removed at autopsy. Gingerly handling the grisly exhibit, Holden identified the teeth and jaws as Olsen's. In addition, Holden identified the pair of wire-cutters which Pennycuick had found in the tent-cabin. They were of the kind issued to all telegraph linemen and, by the pattern of wear on the jaws, Holden was sure these pliers had belonged to Olsen. He was not so sure about the electric belt, testifying that Olsen had indeed worn such a device but that when Holden had seen the belt, it had been covered with fabric. The belt produced in court had no cloth covering.

Captain Fussell and Charles Dorman testified that the three men were traveling together on Christmas Day 1899. This satisfied the court that evidence concerning all three dead men could be used.

Then Wade began the process of tracing O'Brien movements through the testimony of witnesses who saw him at various times and at various places on the river. And in this process, Bruce, the big yellow dog, was central. The dog had already provided the link connecting O'Brien, the prisoner at Tagish, to Miller, the suspected cache thief. The dog had already shown an attachment to the tent-cabin when there was only the stove to place O'Brien there. Now, he would help again because, time after time, people who could not positively identify the accused would, without hesitation, identify the big yellow dog.

Bruce was led into the courtroom for Charles Engquist to see. He recognized the dog. So did Oscar Fogelstrom and Andrew Anderson, the other roadhouse keepers. All three men were reasonably sure of having seen O'Brien before but they were positive about the dog. Agnes Fussell did not know O'Brien at all, although he had been at her roadhouse on 12 December 1899. She did recognize the dog. Captain Fussell remembered the dog very well.

He even knew that the dog's name was Bruce; O'Brien had told him so.

William Levy Powell would only say that the dog was similar to the one he had seen with O'Brien at the Arctic Express cabin. But then, he had more reason to remember the dog's owner. Powell testified that while he and his crew were cutting the overland trail which became known as the Pork Trail, he saw men at the Arctic Express cabin. Powell, having been told he would find hay for his teams in that area, went to the cabin to inquire. O'Brien met him and, as best Powell could recall, said, "There is nothing at that cabin for you and you had better turn back." Powell testified that O'Brien was carrying a pair of field glasses or, more precisely, the case for a pair of field glasses. The case was similar to the exhibit he was shown in court but Powell had never seen the glasses themselves. The witness further stated that O'Brien was carrying a rifle and that his thumb was on the hammer. Powell felt that he was being threatened and did as he was told without delay. Several spectators exchanged knowing looks at this testimony. On cross-examination, however, Powell conceded that when he and James Fetterly went back to the cabin the next day they were received much more hospitably. They were not ordered away. No rifle was seen.

Jennie Prather identified the dog, as did Bayard Burgess, Albert Gibson, Harold Abbott, James Hildebrand and Staff Sergeant Graham. In this way, O'Brien's trail was plotted by a dozen or so people along the river. And no matter what name he happened to be using at the time, it was clear to everyone that the man in the prisoner's box and the big yellow dog had been together from Selkirk to Tagish.

As a final touch, evidence showed that the dog itself was stolen. The real owner, Auguste Mouquin, readily identified the dog as his, stating that the St. Bernard and a smaller black dog had been stolen from him at Dawson in November 1899.

This series of witnesses, however, accomplished more than merely charting O'Brien's route along the river, important as that was. Wade dwelt upon the conversation which took place between the accused and Albert Gibson as they traveled together in the afternoon of 27 December. Gibson clearly recalled O'Brien saying he had left Minto two days before. The witness remembered this because it was so surprising: Minto was only fifteen or sixteen miles behind and Gibson, Bard, and the Prathers had left Fussell's that very morning. Gibson asked O'Brien where he had been for two days and O'Brien replied that he had taken the wrong trail, just as the Prathers had. Gibson had persisted, however, asking if O'Brien had really been lost for two days. The accused had admitted he hadn't, but his dog's feet were worn out and he had stopped to rest them up. Whatever the case, Gibson was sure that the big yellow dog was not lame on 27 December.

And Jennie Prather remembered seeing O'Brien lying on his bunk at Schock's roadhouse on the morning of 2 January 1900. He was counting a roll of bills. She did not know the denominations of any of the bills — the light was too poor for that — but the roll was, she thought, about an inch and a half in diameter. James Hildebrand, too, saw a roll of bills in O'Brien's possession. His testimony agreed with Jennie Prather's: the roll was about an inch and a half in diameter — sort of a loose roll it was — but the denominations were unknown.

Now Wade turned his attention to the physical evidence. He had used people to place O'Brien near Minto in early December 1899. But he was now forced to rely upon the bewildering array of objects through which he hoped to convince the jury that O'Brien had spent the last half of December in and around the tent-cabin, setting his trap.

There was the double-bit axe which had been found in the snow near the tent-cabin. Pennycuick would be able to show most convincingly that the nicks on the blades matched cuts on assorted stumps and logs. There would be little doubt that this was the very axe which had been used to cut the logs for the tent-cabin walls, to cut the swath of trees which blocked the killer's view of the river trail and to clear the rough trails leading to the scene of the murders. But the question was: whose axe was it?

Constables Lynn and McBeth testified that the double-bit axe belonged to George O'Brien. Both were firm in their testimony, claiming to have seen the axe when they recaptured O'Brien after his escape from jail in December of 1898. Both remembered the axe by a split on the handle. Lynn jabbed his hand on the splinter and McBeth claimed to have trimmed the offending splinter off with his knife.

George O'Brien, however, had a different version of the story. In a letter to Inspector Scarth he wrote:

> ... Sept 17th on discharge I found all my outfit was lost. I went and complained to Provost Tweedy ...

O'Brien claimed in the letter that he had then prepared a list of the missing items, which included an axe, and replacements were issued from stores. But, of the replacement axe, he wrote:

> ... Smith found an axe head (single edge) with the handle broke off through use. He gave me a new handle to fit in & remarked to Oaktown 'put this in for him' — I said that's all right I can fix it myself.
> Sir let me ask you to deal fairly with me & don't let them know that McBeth and Lynn have sworn to an axe I never saw or they will deny me justice — respectfully yours.
>
> George O'Brien

George Herbert Tweedy was the man most likely to clarify this matter of O'Brien's axe. He had been the Provost Sergeant in Dawson when O'Brien was first arrested in September 1898, when he was rearrested after escaping in December 1898, and when he was finally released in September 1899. On all those occasions, Tweedy had charge of prisoners' effects.

He identified the .30-30 rifle as O'Brien's, a fact not seriously in doubt, but about everything else he was impossibly vague. There was no written inventory, he said, because books were scarce in 1898; he had to rely on his memory. He remembered only the rifle. The court at last cut off his testimony.

This was just the sort of complication that Scarth wanted to avoid, that he had warned Pennycuick and Maguire about. In an attempt to sort out the tangle, Scarth himself went to the Dawson files and found the inventory of O'Brien's gear. He put it in as evidence. When Tweedy was recalled, he recognized the handwriting on the list as his own but, strangely, still could not explain which items had been lost. On cross-examination, however, Bleeker made three points about the inventory: the robe, which everyone admitted had been lost, had an "X" beside it, the rifle, which everyone knew had *not* been lost, had a blue line through it, and the axe was marked with an "X".

Pennycuick and Maguire spent hours on the witness stand explaining details of the maps they had drawn of the murder trail and showing the signficance of the dozens of articles they had dug out of the snow. One of those items, the mushroomed bullet which Pennycuick dug out of the pool of blood where Clayson had died, was dealt with in some detail. The detectives had found several .40-82 cartridge cases near the scene of the murder and these connected nicely with the rifle left in the tent-cabin. O'Brien, however, carried a .30-30 rifle; there was no evidence to suggest he ever carried any other.

In addition to the rifle cartridges, there were some .41 caliber revolver cartridge cases which corresponded to the weapons O'Brien had in his gear. That was certainly suggestive but scarcely conclusive. The suggestion would be a good deal stronger if it could be shown that it was at least *possible* that the mushroomed bullet was from a .41 caliber revolver. It was obvious that the bullet came to rest where it did only after it had passed through Fred Clayson's head.

Accordingly, Edward Telford, the hospital sergeant, was called. He testified that, at the request of Inspector Scarth, he had extracted the bullets from two unfired cartridges, one a .40-82, the other a .41. He weighed the bullets and found that the .40-82 weighed 260 grains and the .41 weighed 194¾ grains. The mushroomed bullet weighed 195 grains. Telford said that the exhibit *may* have weighed the same as the unfired .41 because when he extracted the bullet from the .41 revolver cartridge, he lost a little lead on the jaws of the pliers.

Scarth was not so reluctant. He testified that in his opinion, based on bullet weights and on the shape of the base of the mushroomed bullet, the exhibit was the slug from a .41 caliber revolver.

Corporal Ryan entered and explained the photographs he took of the tent-cabin and the trails.

James Hildebrand, George Noble, and Florence Lamar made putty models of the double nugget. After Fred Wade had primed the jury in his opening remarks, this testimony left a strong impression. Henry Bleeker saw the importance of the nugget and he pressed all three witnesses in his cross-examination, suggesting that there had been collusion. The witnesses admitted that they had, some time previous, met at the prosecutor's house and had made models of the nugget then. But, each stoutly maintained that his recollection was his own, uncolored by the opinions of anyone else. And each remembered the nugget a little differently. These discrepancies were trifling, however, adding to the credibility of the witnesses rather than taking away from it. In the end, the jury heard that Noble had given the nugget to Relfe and that, early in January 1900, O'Brien tried to sell it to James Hildebrand. Descriptions and models convinced the jurors that the double nugget in each episode was one and the same.

Will Clayson produced the iron drawers from his business safe in Skagway and demonstrated that the keys Maguire and Pennycuick had found did, in fact, operate the locks in the drawers. Fred Wade then produced the black silk mitts which O'Brien was wearing when he was arrested in Tagish. Clayson noted that the two mitts were mismatched but that the left one was similar to the sort his brother had taken along on his trip to Dawson. He testified further that there was a shiny area on the thumb of the mitt which, he suggested, could have come from rubbing on bicycle handlebars. Clayson was probably not entitled to express such an opinion in sworn testimony. But the statement was made and it certainly implied that O'Brien had been wearing the mitts stripped from Fred Clayson's corpse. In his cross-examination, Henry Bleeker could have forced the admission that the black mitts were, after all, of a very common sort and left it at that. He chose, however, to attack Will Clayson's interpretation of the shiny area on the left thumb. Could this not have arisen just as well from contact with the handles of a sled, he asked. Clayson did not immediately back down but argued that sled handles would mark the mitts farther down in the palm. Bleeker persisted, pressing and questioning. In the end, Clayson admitted that he could not say positively that the shiny spot came from contact with bicycle handlebars. But Henry Bleeker knew he had done as much harm as good: the jury, he was sure, would not remember Clayson's retraction nearly as well as they would remember that the shiny spot could have been caused by handlebars. Bleeker's cross-examination had simply imbedded that possibility all the more firmly in the minds of the jurors.

Fred Wade had conducted his case meticulously, anticipating the questions which would occur to the jurors and, wherever possible, answering those questions with testimony. He had identified the dead men, established that they had been shot and showed, as closely as he could, when and where they had died. Then, through the detailed presentation of physical evidence, he had shown *exactly* where the men had died. The wounds on the bodies, the pools of blood in the snow, the mushroomed bullet, the broken tooth, the cartridge cases spoke precisely of how the men had died. The remains of burned clothes and the personal items of no value which had been strewn about the area of the murder trail and the tent-cabin strongly suggested that the bodies had been robbed.

By both eyewitness testimony and physical evidence, George O'Brien was placed near the site of the murders at about the time they took place. The double nugget suggested very strongly that he was part of the enterprise.

The last question Fred Wade anticipated was this: is the accused, O'Brien, capable of such a crime? Certainly, *someone* murdered Clayson, Olsen, and Relfe and O'Brien had the opportunity. Did he have the inclination? Fred Wade had the answer for that question, too.

Chris Williams was called and he told of the offer O'Brien made him in May 1898. When it was put to the jurors that O'Brien had had his murderous scheme in mind for more than a year before putting it into action, the effect was devastating. George O'Brien was practically doomed. When Kid West told the same story in his turn, the court scarcely paid him any attention, which was precisely what the prosecutor had in mind.

In his closing address, Fred Wade again reconstructed the story for the jury. He drew their attention to several points which he had not touched upon in his opening remarks. He was particularly emphatic about the field glasses O'Brien carried. This was not an item, he said, that a traveler often had with him, there being no obvious use for glasses on the trail. A pair of field glasses would be extremely handy, however, if one were hidden back in the bush, peering along a cleared strip through the trees, trying, at a mile's distance, to decide whether a particular traveler was worth robbing. And he used O'Brien's own words to telling effect. O'Brien had told Albert Gibson that he had been two days coming from Minto, a distance of fifteen miles. That statement in itself was a virtual confession, he argued.

When he closed the case for the Crown, Fred Wade was satisfied that the jury had followed the twists and turns of the Crown's case and, after Chris Williams' testimony, were prepared to convict. It would require spectacular defense to change their minds.

But, Henry Bleeker faced an enormous task and the possibilities open to him were limited. He called no witnesses, relying upon argument to move the jury.

"My Lord," he said. "Gentlemen. You see here a man, the accused George O'Brien, who has been the object of attention of two governments in this case. For a year and a half, they have been collecting evidence against him, all their resources being brought to bear against one man who has no money and no friends. He has been forced into this trial with but three weeks in which to prepare a defense against a case which took eighteen months to build.

"He stands here accused of the murder of one man but he is compelled to defend himself against the murder of three men. But, I remind you, gentlemen, that the accused is entitled to have the case proven against him; he does not have to prove his innocence. I submit — with all due respect to my learned friend — that the Crown has not made a case. In defense, therefore, we offer no evidence because there is nothing to refute."

Having said that, Henry Bleeker took the next two hours to refute, point by point, the evidence which the Crown had introduced. The entire case, he said, was circumstantial and it was dangerous to rely on circumstantial evidence. He used the Old Testament story of Joseph as an example. Joseph's coat was stained with blood. Jacob accepted this circumstantial evidence and concluded his son was dead. But was Joseph dead? No, indeed. He later turned up, alive and well, in Egypt. Such were the dangers inherent in circumstantial evidence.

Bleeker insisted that the evidence must be inconsistent with the innocence of the accused. Then he tried to present reasonable alternatives for many of the points the prosecution had made. O'Brien had used other names. Was this a sign of guilt, as the Crown implied? No. The accused had served time in jail and changed his name to avoid the stigma of being known as an ex-jailbird.

Was O'Brien behaving like a man fleeing a crime when he was seen in late December? Hardly. He traveled almost step for step with the Prathers and they were not making spectacular time.

Was there something sinister in the fact that O'Brien had two hundred dollars stitched into his socks? Of course not. It was a step any prudent man might take to guard against being robbed.

And when he went through the ice at Tagish, was he really trying to avoid the Mounted Police post, as the Crown would have it? Or did he simply take the wrong trail by mistake and, when Billy Ensen called to him, break through the ice as he was crossing to the proper road?

When he came to the evidence about the nugget and the testimony of Chris Williams, Henry Bleeker could do little to counteract it. But he was scathing in his attack on Kid West.

"I submit, gentlemen, that the testimony of witness Williams is not worthy of belief. By his own admission, he had known the accused for only a week. Does it seem likely to you that the accused would make such a proposition to a man he had known for such a short time?

"And as for Mr. Kid West, what reasonable man could accept as truth anything he said. You heard my learned friend say that he had been doubtful about introducing such a witness. I commend counsel for the Crown; his doubts were well founded. Mr. Kid is a burglar, a thief, a gambler, a convicted criminal borrowed from another country. There is not a shred of honor to be found in the man. He entered this court a coward at heart and with a lie on his lips. To suggest that any part of his testimony be taken as true is to affront this court.

"In conclusion, gentlemen, I submit that a case such as this, built as it is upon circumstantial evidence and the testimony of men like Mr. Kid West, holds grave dangers for a jury. A false step could make you gentlemen practically the murderers of the accused. I put it to you that it is better that ninety-nine guilty men go free than that one innocent man suffer.

"I thank you for your attention."

The defence did not impress. The jurors, to a man, would have agreed that O'Brien was not required to prove his innocence in any way, either by the testimony of witnesses or by speaking on his own behalf. But, the Crown's case contained too many questions which only O'Brien could answer. Henry Bleeker could suggest alternative explanations for facts which the Crown had introduced, as indeed he had. But the man who *knew* the answers sat in the courtroom, silent. What did O'Brien have to say about the double nugget? What of the stove in the tent-cabin? What of the axe and the uses to which it had been put? What of the blood stain on the sled? What of the yellow dog hair outside the tent-cabin? And, even if it were granted that West was a liar, what did O'Brien have to say about the deal offered to Chris Williams? If these questions would not be answered by the accused, then the jurors were free to make of his silence whatever they liked.

They took one hour and fifty-eight minutes to reach a verdict. At thirteen minutes past midnight, 22 June 1901, the jury found George O'Brien guilty of the murder of Lynn Wallace Relfe. Court was then adjourned until ten o'clock.

When court reopened, counsel for the defense moved for a new trial on the grounds that the court had made a number of mistakes. Bleeker argued that it was incorrect to permit evidence pertaining to Clayson and Olsen to be entered, that the testimony of Williams and

West ought to have been disallowed, that Fred Wade had improperly referred to the accused as "an old and experienced thief," that the court failed to grant postponements when the defense requested them and, finally, that Judge Dugas had erred in his charge to the jury. Judge Dugas promptly answered each point, denied the motion for retrial and passed sentence upon the convicted man.

"George O'Brien, you stand convicted of the murder of Lynn Wallace Relfe. I believe you are rightly convicted. I have no doubt of your guilt. Your crime was one of the most heinous in the annals of criminality. Those men had lives which belonged to them the same as your life belonged to you. Yet, you and your partner, for I believe you were not alone, murdered them in cold blood.

"Therefore, George O'Brien, you are ordered to be taken to the place where you have been confined and there kept until the 23rd day of August when you will be brought to a place within the walls of the jail and hanged by the neck until you are dead. And may God help you."

14
Execution

Now that the trial was over, Inspector Scarth could reflect at leisure on the job the Mounted Police had done. And, on the whole, he was satisfied. The Force had done everything that was expected of it. Order had been maintained, the rule of law had prevailed.

There were only the few days in January 1900 in which the people of Dawson had seriously questioned the effectiveness of the police. Those were bad days, as Scarth well knew, when people truly feared for their lives on the trail. And that alarm would not have spread as it had were it not for the shrieking of the newspapers.

The same papers which had laid full responsibility for the missing men on the Mounted Police now were applauding the outcome of the trial. But the credit, unlike the responsibility, did not belong solely to the police. 'Murder will out,' the papers claimed, as if by some mysterious means, the facts of murder would make themselves known. Scarth knew this was nonsense; the facts came to light because every policeman in the Yukon had done his job well.

Some writers saw the hand of Providence in the case. Scarth would not presume to speak of the strange ways of God. But, if the newspaperman meant that there had been a few lucky breaks in the case, Scarth could only agree. He had thought often of O'Brien's arrest at Tagish. If O'Brien had not gone through the ice, he would not have stopped at the Tagish post. If he had not had the government robe on his sled, he would not have been noticed. And the robe would not have been on the sled at all if the police had taken better care of prisoners' effects in Dawson.

Even this, however, was not pure luck. Staff Graham was an astute policeman. Anyone less thorough would have overlooked the ice-caked robe and O'Brien would have been gone. The Mounted Police would then have faced three murders without the remotest chance of solving them. The uproar then would have been awesome.

But, in the end, the case was solved and O'Brien was convicted. Sixty-three witnesses had been collected, including some like Mrs.

Prather, who had been most reluctant to testify. But these people were no longer Scarth's concern. The witness list also included the infamous Kid West, however, who was anything but reluctant. He was still in Dawson, waiting to be escorted back to Seattle. Scarth had heard stories that West had tried to make some deal with the defense. Details of the proposed arrangement were never clear but nothing from Kid West would have surprised Scarth. So, even now, Scarth could not forget about West; the man nagged incessantly.

On 3 July 1901, he wrote:

> Mr Capt Scarth:
> Dear Sir Ive been thinking about that Whitness fee Proposition and it looks like to me that I am agetting the worst of it all the way throght. Ive Been Protecting Seally ever since Ive Been hear and by so doing I Get worst of it. Now he knew I would not come up hear unless I got the coin for coming and he knew that I wanted $500 Dollars to get a Parole for my Partner and he said at Seattle in the jail in the Present of two men that every Body get fees no matter on what conditions they were Brought. He was acting at Seattle as your agent and he gave Mr. Tim Burke the right to tell me what I would get and what to expect. Ive done all I agreed to and more so I certnley will expect the same from you. I took your word that I would not get the worst of it and Depended on not ageting it. You told me I would get 5 per Day Before the trial and now not. That soldger got $100 one Hundred Dollars and he ain't been in jail near a year and never took the stand, I will expect a square deal for I gave you all the best of it so let me know just what is adoing Before the Consul come up as I will tell him just how things are and Get Good proof for what I tell him. Hopeing you wont take this personal I will close Hopeing for an early reply I reamane yours Respectfulley
>
> KID WEST

West was escorted out of Dawson shortly after, thus putting an end, Scarth hoped, to a most unsavory relationship. But, a week later, West wrote from Skagway:

> Capt Scarth Sir
> We arrived all OK. leave at 6 PM this eavining. Ive had a nice trip But I've Been in Jail in White Horse and Skagway. I dont think that was right But I will pass that. Let me know if

you have done anything in my Behalf yet — hpoeing you wont
delay it any longer then you can Help I reamane yours
Respectfulley
KID WEST

Scarth paid the letter not the slightest attention. Kid West was
back in American territory and no longer a concern of his. With a
sense of relief, Scarth turned his mind to other matters. Dr.
Hurdman was to leave Dawson on 18 August for a long tour of the
continent. The Mounted Police Officers' Mess was to hold a banquet
in his honor. And Scarth himself was to leave. He had finally been
given leave to accept the rank of Captain in the Canadian contingent
of the South African Constabulary.

And there was the final stage of the O'Brien matter — the
hanging — and preparations for that proceeded smoothly. Every
detail was promptly reported in the newspapers.

The *Nugget* recorded that O'Brien was now under the minute-
by-minute scrutiny of the death watch. His head had been shaved.
He wore the striped clothes of the convict. He was given no knife or
fork lest he cheat the law. It remained only for him to confess his
crime and, as 23 August drew nearer, there was no doubt he would
do so.

In the days immediately following the trial, O'Brien had given
the jailers some difficulty, ranting and cursing at anyone who came
near him. It was reported that he claimed to be the Virgin Mary and
thus had the power to lay a curse on any who displeased him. Some
said O'Brien was obviously insane; others said his madness was
faked. All of his bizarre behavior, however, was seen as the infallible
sign of a guilty conscience at work. As the days passed, O'Brien
regained some measure of control and asked that a priest be allowed
to visit him. The request was promptly granted; O'Brien was
showing signs of repentance. He did not, however, confess his crime.
He asked that he be buried by three Irishmen, he wrote a letter to
his brother and asked a reporter to mail it, and he read his Bible
diligently. But he did not confess.

It was reported, however, that the man was clearly weakening
and that, while he took some comfort from the priest's visits, he was
not totally at peace. That was entirely just for, as the *Nugget*
reported, "It were a hollow mockery to think that a man whose
hands are steeped in the blood of at least three of his fellow human
beings could possess the peace of mind accorded one innocent of any

crime and who was likewise upon the threshold of death." O'Brien was reported to have said, "I am condemned to everlasting fire and nothing can save me." The *Nugget* reporter knew that only "full and absolute confession to his spiritual adviser" would give George O'Brien relief from guilt. But there was no confession.

And, as O'Brien's behavior was monitored, the gallows were being built. The original plans had to be altered when it became obvious that the enclosure was too small to contain all the people who had passes to watch the execution. There was a quick change of plans and the enclosure was enlarged. By 20 August, construction was finished and the task of testing the scaffold was scheduled. This was well-attended. Sheriff Eilbeck was in charge of the testing but several reporters, police officers, and invited guests were present.

It was reported that the testing was done by fastening two sacks of oats to the rope — a new, five-eighths Manila rope — and springing the trap. All expressed satisfaction that even with two hundred pounds of oats being dropped ten feet, the 8x8 beam did not bend at all. The rope, however, being new, stretched noticeably. So, the test was repeated, measurements were made and the rope was marked so that O'Brien would be dropped seven and a half feet. The gallows worked beautifully.

Still, only three days from death, George O'Brien did not confess. On 22 August, it appeared that, at last, O'Brien would do his duty to all. He asked for Henry Bleeker. The lawyer, reluctantly, agreed to visit O'Brien and, during the hour of their conversation, hopes were high. When Bleeker emerged from the jail, he was immediately beset by reporters, all eager to hear what had happened. But the lawyer shook his head disgustedly.

"In view of past experiences," he said, "I had no desire whatever to see O'Brien but when I was told he desired to make a confession I did not hesitate to do all in my power to assist in the matter. The first few moments of our conversation were taken up in matters pertaining to his private papers and their disposition, and then he said, 'Mr. Bleeker, I am going to make a confession to you.'

"To make a long story short, his entire talk and conversation was but a rehash of statements previously made time and time again. He insists upon his innocence and refers continually to what he terms his defense. He realizes now that there is absolutely no hope for him whatever and he has begun what he calls a defense of his memory. He intends having all his paper and voluminous writings sent to his brother, who, he says, will tabulate them and publish them to the world, establishing his innocence."

"Mr. Bleeker," a reporter cut in, "Do you think he will confess the crime? He has less than a day to live."

"No," Bleeker replied. "I do not believe O'Brien will confess these murders. But, if he does, it will be solely for the purpose of throwing the guilt upon someone else."

"You seem to have an uncommonly low opinion of the man," said the reporter. "But you did defend him. Perhaps you could just state for my readers what sort of man he is?"

"What do I think of O'Brien? I regard him as a degenerate, but half man and half savage with all the cunning, shrewdness and cupidity attributed to the latter. The instincts of a beast of prey and its thirst for blood were born in him, perhaps inherited, but he can no more help being bad than a good man can help being good."

It was a damning opinion and all the more powerful coming from the man who had defended O'Brien. Bleeker's comments were much quoted but they only supported opinions already widely held. What was still missing was the confirmation from the lips of the condemned man himself. His 'confession' was but another terse denial:

> I deny having murdered F. W. Clayson, Lynn Wallace Relfe, or one Olsen, as charged against me and for one of which murders I am condemned to death. My defense as written by me to be published is true in all particulars. I make this declaration as my last statement on the day previous to the day appointed for my execution and protest with all my power that I am innocent of the crimes charged against me and that I am to suffer for the deeds of others.
>
> George O'Brien

George H. Tweedy
Ino. A. Connor
Witnesses

Nor would O'Brien's last visitors fare any better than Bleeker. The representatives of the press entered O'Brien's cell at 9 P.M. of his last night on earth. There was no confession and none of the earlier raving or cursing. Throughout the half-hour interview he remained composed, talking in clear, well-modulated tones and, on the evidence of the *Nugget* report, "as intelligently and rationally as any sane man in Dawson." And within half an hour of the reporters' departure O'Brien was fast asleep. Yet again the enigmatic O'Brien was not living up to expectations of the stereotyped villain.

All that day, people snooped about the jail yard hoping to hear something from the prisoner, perhaps even to catch a glimpse of him. Many asked to see the gallows but this was not allowed. One man was reported as saying that he had never, in all his travels, seen such unparalleled, morbid, almost fanatical, curiosity.

The curious were present early the next morning, too. Almost one hundred passes had been issued to those wanting to watch the hanging, but only the first thirty-five to arrive were allowed on the scaffold; the remainder had to watch from below. There were, in addition, scores of people who had no passes. They gathered in the street outside the jail, hoping to see something. They did not see anything but they heard O'Brien shouting, cursing the escort which had come to lead him to the scaffold. A Mounted Police patrol moved the loiterers along.

At 7:20 A.M., all those with passes were in place and they saw the grim procession leave the jail. O'Brien was in the midst, his arms strapped at his sides. All were struck by his air of calm indifference, his never-faltering step. His only question, posed in matter of fact tones, was: "How long did it take the other poor fellows to die?" He was escorted up the steps to the scaffold, the noose was fitted and the hangman was about to pull the hood over the prisoner's head. The sheriff interrupted and spoke: "George O'Brien, you are about to enter the presence of your God and I ask you now for the last time to confess your crimes. It is a duty you owe to the judge, the jury and the police and everyone in this community to tell how you murdered those poor boys on that Christmas Day. Are you man enough to do it?"

"Do you want to hear the truth?" O'Brien answered calmly. "I did not murder those men."

"Who did murder them, then?"

"I do not know, nor do I know anything about it."

The sheriff looked at O'Brien for a moment that seemed to last forever, then he snapped his fingers. The hangman deftly pulled the hood over George O'Brien's face, stepped back and sprang the trap.

It was 7:35 A.M., Friday, 23 August 1901.

Bibliography

Indispensable sources of information were: The King vs. George O'Brien, trial transcript, Public Archives Canada; such newspapers as *The Daily Klondike Nugget,* June-August 1901 and *The Dawson Daily News,* January-June 1900; the annual reports of the Royal North West Mounted Police, *Sessional Papers* no. 28 (1901-1902).

In addition the following books and articles were invaluable:

Atkin, Ronald. *Maintain the Right.* Toronto: Macmillan, 1973.

Berton, P. *Klondike.* Toronto: McClelland and Stewart, 1972.

Block, Irvin. *The Real Book about the Mounties.* New York: Garden City Books, 1952.

Chambers, Capt. E. J. *The Royal North-West Mounted Police: A Corps History.* Toronto: Coles Publishing, 1973.

Douthwaite, L. C. *The Royal Canadian Mounted Police.* Glasgow: Blackie & Son, 1939.

Fetherstonhaugh, R. C. *The Royal Canadian Mounted Police.* New York: Garden City Publishing Co., 1938.

Gollomb, J. in *Scarlet and Gold* 18 (1936): 27.

Longstreth, T. Morris. *In Scarlet and Plain Clothes.* New York: Macmillan, 1944.

Longstreth, T. Morris. *Murder at Belly Butte.* Toronto: The MacLean Publishing Co., 1931.

Martinsen, E. L. *Trail to North Star Gold.* Minneapolis: Metropolitan Press, 1969.

Phillips, A. *The Living Legend.* Toronto: Little, Brown & Co., 1957.

Reed, Rev. C. in *Scarlet and Gold* 1 (1919): 15.

Steele, Harwood. *Policing the Arctic.* London: Jarrolds, 1963.

Steele, S. B. *Forty Years in Canada.* Dodd, Mead, 1915; Toronto: McGraw-Hill Ryerson, 1972.

White, G. E. in *Scarlet and Gold* 17 (1935): 37.